E
beyond the Tunnel

Compiled by
Trevor Garrod

Published by Leading Edge Press & Publishing Ltd.,
The Old Chapel, Burtersett, North Yorkshire, DL8 3PB.
☎ (0969) 667566

ISBN 0-948135 50 6

A CIP Catalogue record for this book is available from the British Library.

*This book is dedicated to the memory of the late
Rowland Victor Banks (1905-82),
first President of the Railway Development Society,
resident of Kent and a long-standing campaigner
for the Channel Tunnel.*

Acknowledgements

Compiling this book has been a labour of love and a product of teamwork.

I should like to thank all the named contributors and the photographers whose work we have used. Others who have made useful comments on the text include Ken Davies, Trevor Jones and Gerard Duddridge, while many contributors have also commented constructively on each other's work.

Thanks are also due to Nick Lewis, Eric Barbery, members of the German Railway Society, railway and tourism authorities in the countries described, and, last but not least, Stan Abbott of Leading Edge.

The book is based on continental research and travel, and in some cases residence, by the Editor and his team, over several years. We welcome further comments and news of changes that could be included in a future edition.

Trevor Garrod
1994

Contents

CITY GUIDES

Introduction

The train is a relaxing and civilised way to travel. Now that Britain's railways are linked to those of continental Europe via the Channel Tunnel, the train can take you direct to foreign capitals and fascinating sights through richly varied scenery.

Little more than three hours after leaving London, you can be admiring the Eiffel Tower and cathedral of Notre Dame, or listening to the carillon in the Grand' Place of Brussels. With one change of train at most, you could be sampling wine on the banks of the Rhine or cruising through the canals of old Amsterdam. If your taste is rather for EuroDisneyland, near Paris, that too can be reached by high speed train.

Within 250 miles of the Channel Tunnel portal are five countries whose contrasting history, culture and way of life can be sampled; in cities like medieval Bruges and modern Rotterdam; gracious, 18th century Nancy; and ancient Cologne with its Roman foundations. Trains run past Dutch bulbfields and the rolling hills of Picardy; thread the spectacular gorges of the Rhine, Moselle and Meuse and take you by vineyards and over the wooded Ardennes.

All the places included in *Europe beyond the Tunnel* are on key trunk routes within an easy day's travel of the Tunnel portal.

At many continental stations you can hire a bicycle and explore the surroundings; while buses and, in several cities, trams and metros, connect easily with trains.

So a trip to Europe by land has never been easier. This book will help you to discover it.

PART ONE

FRANCE

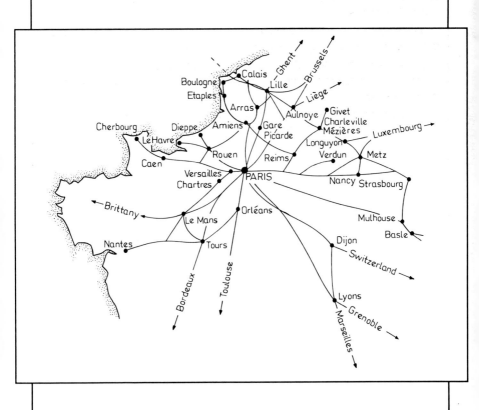

Bruxelles Midi — London — Fréthun — Lille Europe — Paris Nord — Gare Picarde — Arras — EuroDisney & South of France

CHAPTER 1

Tunnel-Paris by TGV

by John Pickford

It will take Paris bound travellers just over 100 minutes to reach their destination after emerging from the Channel Tunnel. During that time they will pass through three regions and seven departments travelling most of the 330km route at a speed of 300km an hour.

The TGV Nord — conceived, built and opened within six years — marks the third phase of the Société Nationale des Chemins de Fer Français (SNCF) Grande Vitesse network. Route planning involved balancing economic and environmental factors, acknowledging agricultural and archaeological lobbies, and protecting the quality of life of the 15 million people living along the route. The outcome has been a massive engineering adventure involving 173 road, 134 rail and 260 watercourse bridges as well as 132 major viaducts.

On leaving the Tunnel, while shuttle trains bear left for the Eurotunnel terminal, Eurostar travellers quickly pass through Fréthun to begin the 113km run through the flat plain of Flanders to Lille. With speed building to 270kph the Calais-Boulogne line is soon crossed and, by the time the A26 motorway from Calais to Arras has been reached, the TGV is cruising at 300kph. Such speed would have been unthinkable for passengers on the infamous ambling Calais-Basle as it plodded through Hazebrouck and on to Lille, the line running parallel to the Belgian border. (See page 25).

This line is crossed by the TGV as it passes the Forest of Eperlecques and the first of the route's six new electricity sub-stations at Ruminghem. Not long after, the monotony of the landscape is broken to the north by rising ground topped by the small town of Cassel. At a modest 176 metres above sea level this picturesque site dominates the surrounding countryside, including the River Aa and the Canal de la Haute Colme, both crossed by the TGV. It is here at Cassel that a link is planned between the TGV line and the classic line from Dunkirk to Arras. This will provide Dunkirk with access via Lille to the TGV network, saving 20 minutes on the time to Paris, for example. Having crossed the classic line, the TGV — still at maximum route speed — passes a major archaeological site at Hondeghem. Here — as at six other sites on the route south of Lille — work has been carried out to protect Iron Age, Roman and Medieval remains. Just to the south of the line at this point is Hazebrouck where classic lines from Lille, Dunkirk, Calais and Arras converge. It is the Lille line which is crossed again shortly before the River Lys as the TGV decelerates through sections at 270 and 220kph before the 200kph approach to Lille. The line will shortly cross the Dunkirk-Lille A25 motorway. Before it does so it passes close to Armentières, a reminder that these are the Flanders fields of sad, poignant First World War memory. The outskirts of Lille are quickly evident with, before Lambersart, the line to the freight depot at Déliverance swinging off to the south. Here the TGV line dives under the classic Dunkirk-Lille line, crosses the Basse Deule Canal and river, and approaches Lille's underground TGV station named Lille Europe. Fifty trains a day stop here, while through-trains for Paris or Brussels cross the central tracks at 200kph quickly to regain the surface.

The city of Lille is described on page 28.

The speed at which the train passes through Lille belies the impact that the establishment of the TGV route has made here, with a massive redesign and modification of the city's railway infrastructure whose classic terminus,

French Railways

The Eurostar carries passengers from London to Paris at an average speed of 300kph

now called Lille Flandre, is France's busiest provincial station. Lines to the coast, Tourcoing, Paris and Baisieux pass over the new line. In this busy railway sector the TGV line passes through Fives and Hellemmes where major maintenance and servicing facilities, along with a central computerised reservation centre, are located.

The section to Lille comprises about a third of the TGV Nord track mileage. Shortly after leaving the city, speed rises to 200kph as the line approaches Fretin. Here the routes to Brussels and Paris diverge. As the TGV Nord bears south at the junction, it crosses the Lille-Valenciennes line and Lesquin, Lille's expanding international airport is visible on the right. Next, the A1 Paris Motorway and the Paris-Lille classic line are crossed. The line is now re-entering the Pas-de-Calais Department and begins to flank the motorway with which it will run parallel for over 100kms at 300kph. While the natural landscape remains essentially flat, man-made tips of coal spoil are dotting the countryside towards Lens to the west and Douai to the east. Mining is no longer active here but all around are reminders of a time not too long ago when coal was king. Trees and other vegetation have been planted — for the environment counts here. Indeed, in the neighbouring areas of Carvin and Libercourt much of the wood at Epinoy has been replaced in line with its protected status. Continuing south, the TGV Nord approaches Arras where various projects are in hand to maximise the operational impact of the new line. North of the town a single track will link the TGV to the Arras-Lille route. This will provide opportunities for traffic originating in Amiens to access the northern sections of the TGV network directly. Further east the single line between Douai and Cambrai will be electrified, putting Cambrai on the TGV map. Finally, south of Arras is the 11km TGV spur, providing access to and from Arras for Paris TGVs. Thus the eastern areas of the Pas-de-Calais will benefit considerably from the passage of the TGV Nord, something that might not have been the case had the route passed more directly to the coast via Amiens.

Amiens, capital of the Somme Department, is a substantial city, many of whose citizens would have liked the TGV to pass directly through it. In fact they will be served by the new Picardy TGV station, situated mid-way between Amiens to the west and St Quentin to the east. The planned A23 motorway will serve the new station. On the approach to Picardy the TGV line crosses the Somme on a 270m viaduct and then passes through a 470m covered section at Assevillers. The scenery is changing as the softer, more rolling landscape of Picardy takes over from the flatter terrain of the North.

None of the landscape crossed so far escaped the terrible impact of the Great War. From Armentières before Lille, through Arras with Vimy Ridge at hand, and now the Somme where 60,000 British soldiers died on the first day of the battle in 1916, the TGV has traversed much formerly contested territory.

South then from TGV Picardy, crossing the Amiens-Laon line and on through Hattencourt to cross the Avre on a short 220m viaduct, the route still parallel to the motorway. One hundred kilometres from Paris the line enters the Oise Department south of Roye. When it leaves the Department in 60kms time it will be running through the outskirts of Paris. It is in Oise that some of the most testing topography has had to be mastered. To cross the river which gives the Department its name, a viaduct 1.5km long had to be constructed graded at one in 40. Once across the viaduct at Longueil the line passes through two consecutive covered sections at Verberie. Before this section the line has crossed the Creil-Jeumont line and parted company at last with the A1.

As Paris gets ever nearer a brief 8km section cuts through the north-east tip of the Department of Seine et Marne. Small though this area is, it is of particular significance for the TGV network. The high speed link between the TGV Nord and TGV Sud Est branches off south at Moussy Le Neuf and passes through the Paris fringes — Roissy-Charles de Gaulle Airport and the Marne-La-Vallée site of EuroDisneyland — before joining the TGV line to Lyon and the South.

The TGV Nord line ends at Gonesse 12kms from Paris on the classic line to Creil and Lille. During the final section the familiar skyline of the French capital is visible as the line traces its way through the busy mix of main line and suburban traffic, past Le Landy facilities and into the TGV terminal at the Gare du Nord.

Lille-Brussels

When the TGV Nord is complete, travellers from Lille to Brussels will hardly have time to take their seats before they are being advised that the train is approaching the Belgian capital's Midi Station. A journey time of 22 minutes is envisaged.

Until 1993, the classic journey by rail remained a mixture of ancient and modern, sedate and brisk. Electrification has now been completed between Lille and Tournai, establishing the possibility of a direct service. However, as yet, despite the improvement in infrastructure, a change at Tournai is still required. What has been lost, however, is the opportunity to sample the delights of a 1970s French diesel unit before being whisked to the Belgian capital by an electric reversible. Such is progress!

This is a journey from French Flanders through Belgian Hainault and Brabant. There is divergence of nationality, culture and language but a uniformity in landscape, here on the fringe of Belgian composer, Jacques Brel's "plat pays". There is time to absorb a countryside whose character is not denied by its lack of the spectacular.

A two-hour service reaches Tournai in just under 30 minutes from Lille.

The onward leg to Brussels Midi is hourly and takes about 55 minutes. Depending on departure times from Lille the whole journey, without a pause to visit Tournai, takes between one and a half and two hours.

The first stages of the journey pass through the increasingly complex rail infrastructure of Lille. Hellemmes, passed after Lezennes, will retain its importance as a rail centre with the operational arrival of the TGV Nord — the extensive works are on the north of the line. Thereafter, the journey to the Belgian border at Baisieux passes through communities both agricultural and commuter — Annappes and Ascq. Tournai lies on the River Escaut not far beyond the border.

The sensible traveller will regard the change at Tournai as an opportunity rather than an annoyance. Two hours would provide a comfortable, unhurried chance to absorb the city's atmosphere and visit its fine cathedral. The station is on the northern side of the city, a 20-minute walk from the historic centre. Tournai was the cradle of the 5th century Merovingian French monarchy and has also been at different periods Austrian and, from 1513-1519, English. Thomas Wolsey was its Bishop. The Five Towers and sheer scale make the cathedral a striking monument. The 12th century belfry, close by, is Belgium's oldest. Tournai most definitely rewards a pause.

From Tournai Belgian Inter City trains serve Leuze and Ath before running fast to Brussels. A change at Ath is necessary for travellers to the intermediate stations of Silly, Enghien and Halle. This local service continues to Brussels, arriving 20 minutes after the direct train.

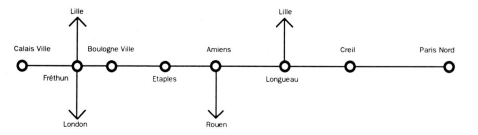

CHAPTER 2

Calais-Paris

The classic route

by Trevor Garrod

The classic gateway to France for ferry travellers from England is the harbour at Calais which separates the industrial zone to the east from the historic town centre to the west. The boat train from Calais Maritime snakes its way slowly out of the docks complex, past the town hall, with its high ornate tower that the boat passengers will have seen as they approached the coast, and into the modernised Calais Ville station.

With a population of 75,000, Calais is an important town and will continue to enjoy through trains to Paris via the classic route. For many years, trains have been diesel-hauled from here to Amiens, where a ten-minute stop was made to change to an electric locomotive; but now this northern stretch of the line is also being wired up.

The train from Calais passes the great complex used by shuttle and freight trains through the tunnel, to reach Frethun, once an insignificant village station. The advent of the tunnel caused it to be resited as part of the network of roads and railways converging on the tunnel portal. Thus you can now alight here from your tunnel train and change for one that will take you into Calais or to Paris via the traditional route and to some interesting towns of Picardy on the way.

Our classic train heads away from the plain of Flanders into the open downland that forms the Boulonnais ridge to the south-west of Calais and meets the sea in the prominent chalk cliffs of Cap Gris Nez. The railway climbs for 13km, mostly at one in 125, curving past the villages of Pihen and Caffiers over a rather bare, rolling landscape not dissimilar to parts of

13

Dorset. It runs through deep cuttings and then descends through the small town of Marquise in a more pleasant, wooded valley, with its modern station and extensive sidings. We then come within sight of the sea once more, as we cross the River Wimereux, with views across the small resort of that name.

Boulogne is soon reached, passing through two tunnels under the town centre to reach Boulogne Ville station. This town of 50,000 people has long been a major port for passengers, cargo and fishing. Shortly after leaving its main station, we cross the River Liane, on the steep sides of whose valley the modern town is built, and which flows down to its harbour. The surrounding countryside is hilly and attractively wooded, while Boulogne has white cliffs to rival those of Dover and a resort quarter with a popular beach and casino.

The line from the harbour trails in on our right, and we run inland somewhat, along a steep-sided valley and past the freight yards of Outreau. But after Hesdigneul the line veers back towards the coast and local trains call at small stations serving Neufchatel and Dannes, the latter village containing some English-looking semis. The sea can be glimpsed as we run past sand dunes to Etaples, an ancient town of 10,000 nestling on the estuary of the Canche. Across the water is the resort of Le Touquet, for many years fashionable with English visitors, its airfield visible on low land by the river. In the 1960s and 70s a rail-air-rail service was operated from London to Paris via Le Touquet, but it became uncompetitive as hovercraft links developed. As our mainline train curves round the back of Etaples and across the river, you can see the single track branch line built in 1963 to serve the airport curving in on the right, its junction now severed.

We now rush south across flat, open countryside with marshland, some stretches of heath, woodland and an increasing number of pools and small lakes. This area was once under the sea, the original coastline being now a few miles inland. We could have changed at Etaples for a local diesel railcar to St Pol, calling at Montreuil-sur-Mer, now several miles from the sea, despite its name.

This is a lightly populated area and some country stations have closed. At Verton, the name remains, picked out in different coloured bricks, on the former station house. We pass gravel pits, many of them now flooded and used for recreation, and can soon spot, among trees to our right, the ornate belfry tower of Rue, a small town served by some of the Paris expresses. Wide marshy flats bring us to Noyelles, where the narrow-gauge Chemin de fer de la Baie de Somme branches off. This runs along the north shore of the bay to Le Crotoy, a small fishing port and family resort, famous for its cockles; and a longer route across the canal to St Valéry, on the southern shore. This small town played a rôle in the preparations for William the Conqueror's invasion of England in 1066. Nowadays its nautical activities are limited to yachting and fishing, thanks to silting up of

Travellers can change at Noyelles for a ride on the narrow guage Chemin de fer de la Baie de Somme to St Valéry from where William the Conqueror prepared to invade England in 1066

the bay in which large sandbanks appear at low tide. The line continues from St Valéry, across flat verdant countryside, to the small resort of Cayeux-sur-mer.

Closed to all traffic in 1969, the lines were taken over by an enthusiasts' group who started to run steam trains for tourists two years later. The service is infrequent and runs only on Sundays and holidays from April to September, and most days of the week in July and August — so you will need to plan your visit carefully. This can be done by asking for a timetable from the Chemin de fer de la Baie de Somme, BP 31, St Valéry-sur-Somme, F80230. The company is very helpful, producing brochures in English as well as French.

We now leave the sea for good, and run inland parallel to the River Somme, again through a landscape that seems to consist largely of marshland, alder and willow trees and lagoons, linked sometimes by waterways, with anglers on the banks or in rowing boats. Small villages are passed from time to time, with their stone churches and cottages with "z" style shutters on their windows. You can spot village cafés advertising Stella Artois, and may recall that a certain Café René is fictitiously set in a small town called Nouvion just to the north of Abbeville, the only significant town on this stretch. The handsome church spire of Abbeville can be seen to our left.

Our rapid progress along the Somme Valley presently brings us to the outskirts of Amiens, described in detail on page 44. All trains call here, and many also call at Longueau, an important station on the outskirts of the city, where the classic route from Arras and Lille joins ours at a great triangular junction.

The landscape gradually changes as we ascend the shallow valley, through Boves, and the farmland turns from pasture to arable, with rolling open fields. Much of what you now see is characteristic of what is generally associated with the French countryside — rows of poplar trees, an ancient chateau among trees...

As we proceed south, however, subtle differences start to reveal themselves. At Liancourt-Rantigny, the sight of the large car park serving the station of this small town tells us that we are entering commuterland. Presently, the line curves down into Creil, an important town and junction with extensive sidings, trees on the steep sides of the valley and modern flats on the hilltops. We cross the River Oise, a tributary of the Seine, and race southwards through increasingly wooded countryside, crossing viaducts over green valleys. The stations look busier, some of them bypassed by fast trains, and many of the station buildings are typical of Chemin de fer du Nord design — a single-storey central section with a three-storey tower at either end, rather like a letter E placed on its side.

Shortly after Goussainville, after passing a line of electric pylons, we can see the TGV line trailing in on our left. By Garges-Sarcelles we are on the edge of Paris, and then pass through suburbs of villas interspersed with trees. As we approach St Denis, villas give way to modern blocks of flats, quite pleasantly situated amid greenery. After passing through the large station serving this suburb you should look out for the first of several views of the great white dome of Sacré Coeur that can be seen between blocks of flats and offices to the right.

The multitude of trains and tracks now running alongside ours heralds the approach to the Gare du Nord, one of the six great termini serving the capital of France.

The Arc de Triomphe — begun by Napoleon Bonaparte to celebrate his victories of 1805-6 and completed after his death in 1835

Paris

Your first visit

by Trevor Garrod

If this is your first visit to the capital of France, you will doubtless want to see its world-famous sights: the Eiffel Tower, the Louvre, the Arc de Triomphe and the cathedral of Notre Dame, to name but a few. You will also want to experience the distinctive streets and boulevards of this city, now just three hours from London, but so very different in character.

Your first exploration of Paris would therefore best be done by bus. A No 42 from the terminal on the eastern side of the Gare du Nord will take you westwards to the Opéra, then down past the beautiful neo-classical church of La Madeleine on to the vast Place de la Concorde on the banks of the Seine. You may then choose to take a walk through the Tuileries Gardens to the Louvre and continue along the banks of the Seine to the Isle de la Cité, on which the city was founded, and which is graced now by the cathedral of Notre Dame.

Alternatively, you may prefer to take a bus up the celebrated Champs Elysées, to the great triumphal Arc de Triomphe in the centre of the Etoile where 12 great avenues meet. Then it could be time for a ride on the Métro, the Paris underground railway built mostly just below street level. Take Line Six in the direction of Nation. This may seem a strange way to see the sights — but it will not seem so strange when your train rises to the surface, and proceeds along the wrought iron viaduct in the middle of the street, soon to cross the river on the unusual Bir Hakeim bridge which it shares with road traffic, but at a higher level. You can continue for five more stations along this elevated section with the sort of views that can nowhere be experienced on the London Underground; or you can alight at Bir Hakeim and stroll a short distance to the foot of the Eiffel Tower, erected on the Champs de Mars in 1889 to commemorate the centenary of the French Revolution.

Now it is perhaps time to enjoy a view across the city. A lift will take you to the first stage of the tower, or you may wish to continue to the second level or right to the summit, 320 metres up. From this great monument, erected to mark the centenary of the 1789 Revolution, you can gaze north-westwards to the futuristic forest of skyscrapers around the unique cubic Great Arch of La Défense, inaugurated in 1989 to mark the revolution's bicentenary.

Turning to the right, across the rooftops to the north of the city, you will see the hill of Montmartre, a bohemian suburb with a village-like atmosphere, dominated by the striking white domed church of Sacré Coeur, built as a mark of national atonement after the French were defeated in the 1870 Franco-Prussian War.

You will doubtless be tempted to inspect both districts at close quarters. But to round off your initial experience of Paris, why not stroll along the river bank to the next bridge, Pont d'Alma, and sample another of the city's pleasures: the Bateau Mouche. Named after a Monsieur Mouche who first introduced them, many years ago, these boats enable you to view the imposing riverside architecture at a leisurely pace and from a different angle, and you can even drink and dine on them as you go.

Paris — a personal recommendation

by Edina Lewis

Over the years Paris does not really seem to have changed since my first visit many years ago (I think I managed a fortnight on £5 all in). It has never lost its instant charm and appeal. Travelling via Newhaven-Dieppe (the cheapest though longest route) I arrived at the Gare St Lazare, in the Quartier Europe (every street named after a capital city) and stayed at the Hôtel de Moscou, rue de Moscou, a charming family hotel, later adopted by the British Communist Party, presumably in a mistaken interpretation of its name.

There have, of course, been changes. For example, Les Halles (the equivalent of London's Covent Garden wholesale market) has disappeared, and you now have the Forum des Halles and the Pompidou Centre (or Beaubourg). But you can still eat scalding hot onion soup at midnight at the Pied de Cochon. Le Marais (marsh) and the rue des Rosiers — the old Jewish Quarter — are still there, but are now part of the regenerated Beaubourg area.

To prepare for your train journey, you will find a wealth of information at the International Rail Centre, Victoria Station, London. Check up about cheap fares in Europe, as these have suffered some cuts recently. The International Rail Centre also provides insurance, which is advisable. Read the small print.

You will find all kinds of information, booklets and leaflets on transport, hotels, restaurants etc at the Maison de la France, French Government Tourist Office, 178 Piccadilly, London W5 9DB.

Of the many guides on the market, perhaps the best and most popular is *Time Out Paris Guide* (Penguin £9.99). *The Michelin Green Tourist Guide to Paris* is very good. My old favourite, *Paris par Arrondissement*, is essential: an excellent street guide — with much other information — invaluable for finding your way anywhere.

There is also an intriguing little book (even if you do not read French) *Paris vu du Bus*, which shows the interesting places to be seen along the main bus routes. Useful publications obtainable in Paris (and some of them at the French Government Tourist Office in London) are: *Time Out Paris Guide* (free — in English), *l'Officiel des Spectacles* (weekly, in French), *Paris le Journal* (monthly, in French), *Paris Selection*, monthly publication of the Office du Tourisme in Paris (in five languages, including English).

An extremely useful source of information, should you have access to it in Paris is Minitel. This is a kind of small personal computer, originally linked up with rail, but now linked up with about everything — post office, theatre, business firms, airlines, and so forth. You can book train, air and theatre seats, check arrivals and departures and obtain printouts of timetables — and even of the Election results.

Here are a few suggestions for places to see, including some less obvious ones: the Sainte-Chapelle (Gothic); Palais de Justice (Law Courts); Musée Marmottan (a little less crowded than some) — superb Manet room; le Marais (marsh); Butte Montmartre; Forum des Halles, with new precinct and gardens (near St Germain l'Auxerrois Church); Buttes-aux-Cailles; La Madeleine and its famous church of St Mary Magdalen with its Greek temple (which in 1837 narrowly missed being chosen as the site for the first railway terminal in Paris) — don't miss the charming flower market; the Marché aux Puces (flea market) — open Saturday, Sunday and Monday; the cabaret le Lapin Agile (named after its one-time proprietor Andre Gill) — once the haunt of famous writers and artists.

For museums and art galleries, first get your monuments and museums pass (Carte musées et monuments). This will enable you to go in without queuing. Leaflet with details obtainable at French Government Tourist Office. A "must" is the Musée d'Art Juif (Jewish Art Museum), Montmartre Jewish Centre; Musée d'Art Moderne de la Ville de Paris (National Museum of Modern Art); Musée d'Arts d'Afrique et d'Océanie (Museum of African and Oceanian Art); Bagatelle (Park and Chateau); Hotel Carnavalet — Renaissance mansion with historic collections of Paris and the Revolution; Cité des Sciences et de l'Industrie (The City of Science and Industry called La Villette) with planetarium; Hotel de Cluny and Museum of Decorative Arts and Medieval tapestries — especially The Lady and the Unicorn; Quai d'Orsay (Impressionists); Palais de la Découverte; Picasso Museum, Hotel Sale, 5 rue de Thorigny; Rodin Museum; Zadkine Museum. Little known but worth a visit is the Musée des Transports Urbains near Porte Dorée Métro station at 60, Avenue Ste-Marie, F94160 St-Mandé.

If you need a rest, sit a while in the Parc Monceau, the Parc Montsouris or the Jardin des Tuileries.

Some interesting museums and galleries outside Paris: Auvers-sur-Oise; Musée Daubigny; Chantilly — Chateau et Musée de Condé; Chartres — Musée des Beaux Arts; Chatenay-Malabry — Maison de Chateaubriand; Compiègne— Chateau; Ecouen — Musée National de la Renaissance; Giverny — Claude Monet and Musée Américain; Jouy-en-Josas — Musée de la Tolle de Jouy; Louveciennes — Parc de Morly; Malmaison; Saint-Germain-en-Laye — Prieuré; Sèvres — ceramics.

Don't forget the green-roofed Gothic Basilica of St Denis, ancient place of pilgrimage and burial place of the last Kings of France. Full of history, it is situated at the end of a Métro line, but also accessible by suburban train from the Gare du Nord and a newly opened tram link from the new suburb of Bobigny.

Transport

There are three main public transport networks:

Métro: This is perfectly safe, but you may prefer not to travel alone after 9 pm on lines where there are long pedestrian corridors to negotiate between different lines. Far clearer and better labelled than the London underground.

RER: (Réseau Express Régional) : A banlieue (suburban) 'Métro' going through Paris. Roughly equivalent to London's Thameslink. Stations are generally further apart than on the Métro and so the RER is often the quickest way to travel longer distances.

Bus: By far the best way of getting your bearings in Paris and seeing things you would miss by Métro — though generally, alas, buses do not run late in the evening. Bus stops (unlike those in London) make it clear which direction you are going.

Bus and Métro each has its own "carnet" of ten tickets, but better to have a Paris Visite pass. The same pass covers Métro, bus and central RER zones. As it is zoned, it is better to take the central zone pass and pay the occasional supplement, rather than one covering all zones out to remote suburbs. It can be bought at all major Métro stations.

RATP: (Régie Autonome des Transports Parisiens) is equivalent to London Transport. All airports have an RER office or connections. Maps and tickets are obtainable at all Métro stations (ask your hotel where the nearest one is). Information on tickets etc is available at French Government Tourist Office.

Boat trips: Don't forget to take a boat trip along the Seine, by Batobus, Bateau-Mouche or Bateau Parisien.

If you are also taking in EuroDisney, you may wish to stay in the new town of Marne-la-Vallée. There are good hotels there and it is easy to commute to Paris by RER.

Coming nearer in, though not to the heart of Paris (which is not essential), my friends who live in the 17th arrondissement (district or borough) say that this is a good district to stay in: quiet, with good hotels and restaurants and excellent bus and Métro services to the centre. The quarters around the Gare du Nord and other mainline stations also contain plenty of hotels in various price ranges.

For food, look for the places where French people are eating. The cheapest places are ethnic — such as Chinese, Vietnamese or Moroccan — and pizzerias. All EuroDisney food (fast or not) is excellent, but not cheap. If you are a cheese addict, do visit Androuet, 41 rue d'Amsterdam, 8e, chock-a-block from cellar to roof. You can have a cheese salad (nothing but cheese), or you can eat your way through all the cheeses, from the mildest to the strongest .

The best way to see Paris is on foot. Apart from the walks suggested in the guide books, a good way is to walk from one end to the other of one of the main streets or Boulevards, such as rue St Honoré, rue du

Faubourg St Honoré or Boulevard Haussman. They stretch for miles, without a change of name.

EuroDisney, east of Paris and served by RER, has become a major attraction for families visiting the city. An alternative to this American import is the very French Parc Astérix, set in 350 acres of woodland 38km north of Paris. It can be reached on the RER line to Roissy-Charles de Gaulle Airport and then by 20 minute shuttle bus.

The attractions centre on the cartoon character Astérix the Gaul and his conflicts with the occupying Romans, but there are also less ancient topics such as an audio-visual display on the construction of Notre Dame Cathedral.

The great termini

by Trevor Garrod

Six great termini were built in the 19th century for the main line railways, or "grandes lignes" as the French call them, radiating from Paris to all parts of the country. If you are travelling onward from Paris into the provinces, you will no doubt wish to use one or more of them. Five of them remain essentially in their grandiose classic form, with only Montparnasse totally rebuilt. It is worthwhile to look around the terminus before you start your journey, for each is an architectural monument in its own right.

The Gare du Nord preserves its façade of classical symmetry, adorned by the columns and statues, while behind it is the high functional trainshed supported on square stone pillars and cast-iron columns, much as it would have been in steam days.

However, the eastern side of the station has now been converted to the "Gare de Londres" for the Channel Tunnel trains. An underground car park for 1,300 vehicles has been built while bureau de change and tourist information office are also near at hand.

In this, as in other termini, watch for the signs "Grandes Lignes" (for inter-city trains) and "Banlieue" (for suburban services); though some of the latter no longer use the surface station but run into the RER tunnel and call at subterranean platforms instead.

The frontage of the Gare de l'Est has also changed little from when it was built. Presiding behind iron railings and a cobbled court at the head of the Boulevard de Strasbourg, its dignified stone façade contains shields of the towns and cities served, while statues representing Strasbourg and Verdun grace the entrances of the departure and arrival halls respectively.

The interior is clean, light and airy, with electric trains waiting at any of the 28 platforms to speed you to Champagne, Lorraine and Alsace, or across the border to Luxembourg, Germany or Switzerland.

There are poignant reminders of the past: the departure hall contains a large 1986 Painting of First World War soldiers leaving for the Front, while on the concourse are memorials to the prisoners of war and deportees who passed through this station, as well as to the railwaymen who lost their lives in hostilities.

French Railways

The magnificent classical façade of the Gare du Nord

The Gare de Lyon is on a rather cramped site just off the Boulevard Diderot, its narrow but high façade dominated by a distinctive clocktower. Inside it looks a little untidy and grimy, but it is the starting point for TGVs to the French Alps, the Riviera, the vineyards of Burgundy and the great cities of Dijon, Lyon and Marseille. Its 19 platforms are mainly used by long-distance trains; the Paris-Lyon-Méditerranée Company which built it did not have a large suburban network. Some of the suburban trains use underground platforms and you will also find a suburban ticket office and shops there; while in 1996 a new "météor" underground line is due to serve this terminus. Back at ground level, note the beautiful wrought-iron work in front of the famous "Train bleu" buffet.

If you are using the Gare d'Austerlitz, take Métro line five. The train emerges into daylight at Quai de la Rapée, climbs sharply, executing a 90 degree turn, before rattling across the Seine and over a tree-lined embankment to plunge through the wall of the terminus.

Trains from here do not go to Austerlitz — that is a small town in what is now the Czech Republic, where Napoleon won a famous victory over Russia and Austria in 1805. The Gare d'Austerlitz was the terminus of the Chemin de fer d'Orléans, whose name can still be seen carved on the façade, along with symbolic figures of Nantes, Tours,

23

Bordeaux, Périgueux, l'agriculture and l'industrie. Trains leave this station for the Loire Valley, the west coast, the Pyrenees and Spain.

The Chemin de fer d'Orléans also wanted a more central station and, in 1900, completed a route, now used by RER trains, to the Gare d'Orsay on the riverbank, opposite the Tuileries gardens. However, for various reasons, long-distance traffic continued mainly to terminate at "Paris-Auster" (for short) and the former Gare d'Orsay is now an art museum containing Impressionist paintings formerly housed at the Orangerie des Tuileries.

The Gare d'Orsay is now home to some of the country's finest Impressionist paintings

Continuing our clockwise progress, we next come to Montparnasse, the only rebuilt terminus in Paris. It was reconstructed in the 1960s and its glass frontage is slightly reminiscent of the Pompidou Centre, with escalators between the various levels. Like other Parisian termini, however, it is adorned with the names of towns and cities served — in this case the segment from Granville in the north to Nantes in the south, encompassing the cities of Chartres and Le Mans, the lower Loire Valley and all of Brittany. TGVs to the South West also start from here. Travellators will take you from the main concourse to the Vaugirard suburban section of the station — beyond which you can view the sleek grey TGVs emerging like greyhounds into daylight to begin their swift journey towards the Atlantic Coast.

Our round trip finishes at St Lazare, a large 27-platform terminus in the north-west central area, hiding behind its hotel. It serves Normandy and, by extension, England, through the ports of Dieppe, Le Havre and Cherbourg. The hero of one of J K Huysman's novels in the 1880s went in search of England, wallowed in the anglophile atmosphere of the station restaurant and then called off his trip to London, declaring that, after this station, all else would be an anticlimax.

Nowadays, this terminus is served by electric suburban and long-distance trains, and its restaurant is as French as any other. There is a good range of shops on its high-level concourse and in the ground-level gallery below. By the end of the century, it should also have further subterranean platforms serving a new RER-style link from the Gares de l'Est and du Nord — where we started our tour.

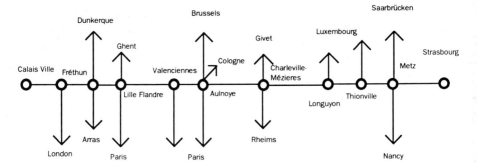

CHAPTER 3

From the Tunnel to Strasbourg

The Portal to Calais and Lille

by Gerard Duddridge

On emerging from the Channel Tunnel portal at Sangatte we arrive at the TGV station of Fréthun. On our right are the through lines, London-bound platform and station buildings. Reached by subway and parallel to us on the left are the new platforms for the old Calais to Paris line. This route, on its way to Boulogne, passes beneath the high speed line and immediately restarts its ascent to surmount the chalk hills.

Those changing for Calais will set off west, but then return north to pass alongside the complex of terminal buildings which include the customs facilities for freight and the vehicle shuttle line on the far west. Within a few minutes the junction of Fontinettes is reached and trains curve in to join the original 1846/48 line from Lille. The line skirts the edge of St Pierre, the commercial/industrial area of Calais, where lace, introduced from Nottingham in 1818, used to be the traditional industry. The original station was on the north side of the town and served the harbour as well, but was superceded after extensive enlargement of the latter, at the beginning of the century. Since that time the line has curved into Calais Ville on the south side and has continued as a harbour branch to Calais Maritime.

Calais, the nearest seaport to Britain, has had a turbulent history, being occupied by the English from 1347 to 1558, by the Spaniards in 1596 and finally, save for the last world war, returned permanently to France in 1598 following the Treaty of Vervins. The dominant building visible from the train is the Hôtel de Ville situated in the Place d'Armes and built in 1740. The imposing clock-tower is earlier though and is 15th century, while Rodin's sculpture depicts the Burghers of Calais. Sand dunes characterise the coast and Sangatte, just 8km to the south west, marks the start of them, the chalk having dipped deeper than 100m below Calais, so leaving its buildings resting on just sand and clay. The dunes form a protective barrier to the low flat lands so characteristic of Flanders. The dune coast can be followed by train to Dunkirk (Dunkerque in French), but only in summer do some trains cross the border via Bray Dunes into Belgium, because regular services ceased from the end of March 1969.

Continuing east on the high speed line to Lille, which will be reached in 30 minutes, we hug the northern margin of the chalk hills towards St Omer, while the old line is about 8km to the north and close to the Calais to St Omer Canal. For Paris the chalk was a barrier to the early construction of a direct line via Boulogne so that trains then travelled via Lille. History seems to be repeating itself, particularly if the high speed cutoff line via Amiens is built. At about 25km from Fréthun we are only 2.5km away from the World War II Eperlecques launch site for the V1 and V2 rockets. To our right is the forest of Eperlecques and then we sweep on to the 2km long viaduct to take us across the river and canal of Haute Colme. We are briefly on the levels drained in 1169 under the instruction of Philip of Alsace and we see them stretching away to the north towards Dunkirk. The poorly consolidated ground has here necessitated deep 35 to 45m foundations for the viaduct.

Looking to the south on our right we see the hill at Watten and the old line which follows close to the left bank of the Aa to St Omer. The river here forms an important link in the canal system. St Omer has been French since Louis XIV captured the town in 1677 — it previously belonged to Flanders. Of note is the 13-15th century basilica as well as the art gallery, river traffic and attractive riverside gardens. The town is served by the old line from Calais to Lille.

Fifty kilometres from Fréthun, the line passes to the south of the small hill top town of Cassel, the first of the Monts de Flandre which are on our left for the next 20km. Cassel celebrates the festival of the Mill on the French national anniversary, July 14. The mill was only built in 1948, but replaces one which stood from 1564 until burnt down in 1911. Within a few minutes the important freight and passenger branch to Dunkirk is crossed and a junction allows trains to run on to the high speed line. This branch joins the old main line at Hazebrouck and, until November 1980, carried through Night Ferry Wagon Lits sleeping cars from London to Paris and Brussels. For the winter sports traffic, a through coach was experimentally run from London to Basle until the end of February 1969.

At 70km we cross the old line and approach the Dunkirk-Lille motor-way. Passing to the south of Armentières, the River Lys and its parallel canal is crossed, but on approaching Lille at Lompret we are once again on the north side next to the old line. Between Lambersat and Saint-André crossovers are provided which can take trains round the north side of the town to approach the terminus Lille Flandre from the east. However, the high speed line carries straight on, passes under the old line, crosses the Deule Canal on a viaduct and then tunnels to reach the through high speed Lille Europe station, situated 400m north of the terminus, 101km from Fréthun.

Lille with Roubaix and Tourcoing is an industrial metropolis and a frequent tram service links these towns from the terminus station, though there are SNCF services as well some of which cross the border to Ghent and Antwerp (Anvers).

Lille

by John Pickford

For Lille, 1993 marked the final act of its consecration as the first European metropolis. Here it was in 1987 that President Mitterrand and Prime Minister Thatcher signed the treaty inaugurating work on the Channel Tunnel, and it was through Lille that trains to Paris and Brussels passed in 1993 with the completion of the TGV Nord. Lille's Mayor, Pierre Mauroy, President Mitterrand's first Prime Minister, was determined that both ventures should benefit '.is city and so they have.

21st century Lille sees itself as the hub of Northern Europe. Less than 350kms distant are Paris, Brussels, London, Luxembourg and the Hague; with journey times of 57 minutes to Paris, 25 minutes to Brussels and 90 minutes to London. Lille with its population of a quarter of a million is finding itself at the heart of an urban community of four million and at the epicentre of a European agglomeration of 70 million. So it is that this city of rich cosmopolitan heritage and tradition gives concrete expression to the reality of the European ideal.

Lille has always been a crossroads: a city of change and development invariably swept along by the tides of European industry. Flanders has been French since 1667. Previously Burgundian, Austrian and Spanish Hapsburgs held sway. In 1914 and 1940 began four-year periods of German occupation. Both wars saw human loss and physical destruction. Lille survived both ordeals, reflecting the spirit of independence and resistance given expression by Charles de Gaulle, born in Lille in 1890.

During the last century, Lille has seen its historic rôle as a centre of textile manufacture disappear. Today, while architects like David Avital sensitively renovate former mills and workshops, and Pierre Louis Cartier works to restore old Lille, its future lies in the service sector — now employing 75 per cent of the workforce — and the hightech industries of Villeneuve d'Ascq, the flourishing "technopole" of the 1970s. As such Lille offers a wide spectrum of attractions to visitors in a hurry, or with time to spare in the area. Organised walking tours cover an architectural heritage which reflects Lille's turbulent and varied history. Within easy reach of the station are L'Hospice Comtesse and the Palais Rihour, both dating back to the 15th century. Representatives of the 17th century are the Old Stock Exchange, originally built in 1662 under Spanish influences, and Vauban's Citadelle, completed in 1698 to secure Lille once-and-for-all for France and Louis XIV. The Portes de Paris and de Roubaix recall a once-walled and vulnerable community. Two hundred years later industrialisation was generating a fresh expansionist spirit reflected in the civic pride of buildings such as the Préfecture of 1869 and the Palais des Beaux-Arts, finished in 1892. The 20th century has given us the Nouvelle Bourse (1920), the Town Hall (1925), the Beffroi (1932) and, from the period of post-war regeneration, the Cité Hospitalier (1956).

More recently, and thoroughly in keeping with its self-proclaimed high-tech image, Lille has developed the VAL: the fully automatic, driverless metro/rapid transit system. Opened in 1983, Professor Gabillard's brainchild comprises two lines radiating from the station. By the year 2000, further expansion of the network is planned towards and beyond the Belgian border. Speeds of upto 80kph, trains that can operate at one-minute intervals and smooth interchanges with other forms of surface transport have made the VAL system a winner. From Bordeaux to Chicago, from Strasbourg to Florida, the VAL has made its point.

Visitors to the system should find time to admire the work of local architects and designers who are responsible for many of the works of art at various stations, most notably perhaps at République.

Lille therefore offers much to visitors with just enough time to sample the town itself. Within striking distance and accessible by train for those with a day or two to spend in the area, are: Bavay, a Gallo-Roman settlement; Le Quesnoy with its own Vauban fortress; the historic Le Cateau and Lewarde with its mining museum, well-served by public transport from Douai station. Douai itself, along with Armentières, Arras and Béthune, provide interesting rail-based day or short break opportunities. With the impact of the TGV, day trip opportunities will include Brussels, Paris and beyond but the Nord itself remains the heartland that Lille services, where a distinctive Nordiste atmosphere will survive.

Before 1994 train passengers arrived at a station with roots in the steam age. The Chemin de Fer du Nord opened to Lille in 1846, and within four years routes to Calais, Dunkirk and Ghent were available. (The façade of the SNCF station dates from 1867.) TGV services to Lyon started in 1984 and were an immediate success, adding to the traffic which had already made Lille France's busiest provincial station. Tunnel and TGV Nord passengers arrive at the new TGV station, built as part of the massive Euralille development. While through services to Paris and Brussels will pass through the station at 200kph, 50 trains a day will be stopping at Lille. The new complex, which includes the underground TGV station, also comprises the Triangle des Gares, the Cité des Affaires, the Portes de Romarin, the Congrexpo and the Parc Urbain, in all a 50-hectare site developed to provide a focal point for the opportunities created by 1994. Amid all this, a link with the past has been maintained in that TGV Nord and Trans Manche will be serviced at Hellemmes Works which opened in 1893, produced its final steam locomotive in 1965, and has operated as a major element in the SNCF electric system since.

Lille will be host to increasing numbers of visitors after 1994. Whenever they arrive, in May for the Foire, in September for the famous Braderie or for the Festival in October and November, they will find a warm welcome from a people noted for its hospitality. Here is a place to eat and drink well and to enjoy good company; to sample waterzoi, potjevleish, hochepot and goyère in restaurants as chic as L'Huîtrière and as simple as Wazemme's Le Breton; to taste some of the many local brews in this homeland of beer; to remember that it was while working on fermentation for local breweries that Pasteur discovered microbiology; to recall that it was here that for the first time in 1888 the *Internationale* was sung. Lille is singing it to a different tune in 1994 — the city that cherishes its heritage and is grasping the future with enthusiasm.

Calais to Metz — the last frontier

by Michael Oakley

From the time that modern France began to establish itself, between the fifth and tenth centuries, certain natural frontiers have always been evident. The seas on the west and south-east, the mountain masses of the Pyrenees and the Alps to the south, and, in the north-east, the Rhine Valley. In the north, however, there is no such clear boundary. Here the open agricultural lands of Picardy shade into the levels of Flanders and the border with Belgium picks its way aimlessly across the flatlands around Lille, clips the bottom edge of the Ardennes forest area and skirts just clear of Luxembourg and the Saar. Only when it reaches the Rhine, opposite Karlsruhe, does it meet a natural frontier and one which has been much fought over.

The cross-country railway route from Calais follows a similarly piecemeal course — indeed, it is only in recent years that this route has emerged as the principal one. Previously cross-country trains tended to follow the Paris route as far as Amiens then struck across the Champagne country to Rheims and on to Basle. However, when major new electrification work was undertaken after the Second World War as part of France's recovery programme, the situation changed. Electrification was bestowed upon the more northerly route near to the Belgian border and the Rheims route has today lapsed into branch-line status with residual diesel working.

Indeed, in spite of the hype which surrounds its major new railway achievements, France remains a country with remarkably little electrification, (12,430km out of a network of 30,909km in 1989). Even this was done in a noticeably piecemeal way, the principal project being the Valenciennes to Thionville section. This was much more a freight than a passenger objective, as was the subsequent extension of the wires to the freight port of Dunkirk rather than the passenger terminal of Calais. Only with the opening of the Channel Tunnel did the all-electric journey become possible; the portion between Calais and Lille remaining diesel-worked to the last, on two through trains a day.

For any rail journey across France, other than through Paris, these two Calais to Metz trains provided most people's only other option. In October 1993, the service was cut back to Lille, and it remains to be seen whether it will be developed into a useful connection for trains from London. The trains' afternoon departure time (summer extras tend to depart even later) made it important to consider how much daylight would be left if all the route was to be seen properly — though in the other direction the times worked out better. The train formations could also vary considerably with the seasons, anything from four to ten vehicles, though mostly now of modern Corail stock. One of the standard medium-sized SNCF diesels would provide the motive power as far as the first reversal at Lille, with a fast level route giving it plenty to do with a maximum load.

The town of Calais and its vicinity are described in Chapter 4. From Calais the classic line at once turns sharply inland and the scenery becomes completely flat and agricultural. Flemish influences are apparent in the names of the wayside stations, and only far away to the south is the flatness broken by a line of low hills.

The first sizeable country town encountered is St Omer, where there are also brief views of the waterway system that extends to the north. The town is noted for its basilica and art gallery, while boats on the waterways pass through attractive gardens. The next major station is Hazebrouck, junction with the main line from Paris and Arras, and Dunkirk. Flat open fields continue to be the norm throughout this section, except for the growing industrial town of Armentières which gained unfair notoriety with the wartime song, *Mademoiselle from Armentières*.

On quite a different scale is the city of Lille, capital of the Nord department and a major industrial centre. The train's winding approach through Lille's urban sprawl, which stretches virtually all the way to the Belgian border, gives the passenger an opportunity to appreciate the sheer size of the city. Time is needed to seek out the fine historical buildings to be found here — described earlier.

The Metz train departs from Lille behind an electric locomotive, probably one of the 1958 16000 series. As the countryside becomes a little more populated after St Amand-Raismes, we will see more frequent local services and glimpses of a large forest area to the north. Otherwise plain farmland continues to Valenciennes, birthplace of the painter Watteau but a very different place from the artist's day with its increasingly industrialised character. The station building on the right is worthy of attention, a large red brick central building flanked by two equally impressive ones to either side. The complex of lines around Valenciennes reflects the importance of coal mining in the area.

In a land where so much has been razed by successive wars, Le Quesnoy is an attractive survivor, with its moated fortifications from many centuries ago. We pass through the Forest of Mormal and, at Aulnoye, intersect the main line from Paris to Brussels and Cologne. The landscape now gradually becomes a little more rolling, the line of the railway a little more winding, and speed will be held around 75mph for much of this distance. We are climbing gently into the foothills of the Ardennes, with patches of forest noticeable to the north. At Fourmies we see the first major civil engineering structure of the route — a river viaduct and approach embankment giving views over the town from the west.

Another country junction is Hirson. This used to be the terminus of a through service from Paris, and trains still slow down at the curve as if to remind us that this used to be the more important flow. After Liart comes the line's first tunnel, as we cross a corner of Picardy and enter the Champagne region. A second tunnel marks the watershed between westward drainage towards the Channel and streams that flow eastwards towards the Meuse. The line descends again to the valley of the Meuse, still winding steadily among straggling bits of the Ardennes forest. Distantly visible to the south-west is the Thiérache, a cattle-farming area noted for its fortified churches. The population is thin again here, and even the indulgent SNCF has given up and closed every intermediate station. Less than perfect track makes this the slowest part of the run in spite of electrification.

At last we reach Charleville-Mézières, where we reverse at the junction with the line from Paris via Rheims. This is one of the few places where the French indulgence for multi-barrelled place-names is inarguable, since Mézières dates from medieval times and occupies the south bank, while the relatively more recent Charleville is laid out on the north. A notable son of Charleville was the poet Rimbaud. From this point we will most likely have taken on one of the newer 15000 series electrics, and the restart gives a good view back across the twin towns from the bridge over the Meuse. It is worth breaking your journey here, however, to explore the town, whose Place Ducale, with its arcaded tall-roofed houses, is most attractive. You can also catch a local diesel train for a scenic 64km run northward along the Meuse valley to Givet. The river meanders are deeply incised into the Ardennes massif, and the railway follows first one bank and then the next, tunnelling through spurs between some of the loops. The Belgian village of Treignes, 5km to the west of Vireux-Molhain station, is terminus of the "Three Valleys Steam Railway", (see chapter 7).

Continuing towards Metz, we reach open countryside again, the wooded hills having receded to the north-east, though they remain visible in the distance on both sides. A curiosity, then, that this should be such a strategic location in military history. The river curves round with the track to reach Sedan, now much industrialised but still boasting the largest castle in Europe. It was here in 1870 that the Second Empire was brought to collapse at the hands of the Prussians. Prior to the Second World War, Sedan was a key fortification on the northern part of the abortive Maginot Line. Rather older fortifications survive at Montmédy, where the line crosses into Lorraine and climbs once more over rolling countryside. A half-mile tunnel takes the line under the castle.

At Longuyon, which nestles under a wooded hillside, the line crosses its summit. Luxembourg is not far away and is served by a branch line. This is another route that has been demoted in recent years, only remnants surviving of the through Paris-Rheims-Charleville-Luxembourg services. Today the longer but faster Est main line takes them round into Metz from the south, then on to Luxembourg via Thionville. Here the Calais trains, having crossed the rich north-south iron ore field east of Audun-le-Romain, curve round to meet the Paris-Luxembourg trains going the other way at the heavy industrial town of Thionville in the vale of the Moselle. Thionville station is at the north point of the triangular junction, and most trains avoid having to reverse there by calling instead at Hayange.

The five-hour journey from Calais comes to a halt, if not an end, in Metz, capital of the Moselle department. Here a large modern town has grown up around the old, the latter dominated by its Gothic cathedral. The satirist Rabelais was town physician here — one hopes not ironically. Metz station is the main point for train remarshalling, with trains on the Brussels-Luxembourg-Strasbourg-Basle route gaining and shedding portions. Through coaches operate by this route through Switzerland to Italy, while connections are possible with Paris to Frankfurt services. Finally, to the south of Metz lies its sister city of Nancy, with the extensive Regional Nature Park of Lorraine on either side.

This is a route of subtle contrasts, which, like much of France, reveals more of itself the further one explores.

CHAPTER 4

Travelling on the TGV

French Railways

Paris to Grenoble

(THE SUD-EST LINE)

by Martin Thorne

The Train à Grande Vitesse, which first entered service on the Sud-Est high-speed line (Paris-Lyon) in 1981, has been a fabulous success. It has taken over half the business from the French internal airline, Air Inter, and services from Paris (Gare de Lyon) have been expanded to include Lausanne and Geneva in Switzerland, Nice and Montpellier in the South of France and of course Grenoble at the foot of the French Alps, the route of which is described in this chapter.

At the Gare de Lyon, the station is divided into arrival platforms, departure platforms and TGV platforms (which are located below ground). TGVs use both their own platforms and departure platforms (check when you arrive at the station). The departure platforms are reached via the ticket hall.

On departure from Gare de Lyon, the TGV passes the Conflans servicing depot (the TGV's own servicing depot is behind here) before running out into the Paris suburbs. For the first 15 miles or so the TGV runs on the original main line to Lyon before joining its own purpose-built high-speed line (note the rapid increase in speed!).

For the first 100 miles or so the high-speed line passes through fairly level countryside in the Department of Seine et Marne where Brie cheese is made.

After the high-speed branch to Dijon leaves the main line, it gradually becomes more hilly (for train enthusiasts, the trackbeds of several disused railways are crossed, including one disused narrow-gauge line complete with viaduct). The line now enters the Burgundy region of France, famous, of course, for its wines, and passes the purpose-built TGV station at Le Creusot, served mainly during peak hours. The high-speed line now starts a stiff climb towards its highest point, at 3,500 metres. As the TGV approaches the summit it slows to 137 mph to avoid derailing at the top. The TGV now starts to descend towards Lyon, passing the second purpose-built TGV station at Mâcon, again mainly used during peak hours and which serves the wine producing areas nearby, notably Beaujolais.

The countryside flattens out again before the TGV approaches Lyon. Just before the high speed line rejoins the old main line from Paris is the junction for the Lyon TGV bypass line. This line will be used by TGVs heading for the Riviera and includes a station at Lyon Airport (plans to extend the high-speed line beyond Valence, where the TGV bypass line rejoins the original main line, to the Riviera at Marseille, have run into large-scale environmental opposition and will probably not be completed in the near future).

At Lyon the TGV calls at Part-Dieu station, built in 1983 to facilitate easier interchange between TGV, local trains and municipal public transport and which also has a large car park. TGVs terminating at Lyon continue for a mile or so further on before ending their journey at Lyon-Perrache, Lyon's original station, which was also modernised for the TGV. The TGVs heading for the Riviera do not stop usually in Lyon.

After Lyon Part-Dieu the line splits into three: to the right it leads into Lyon-Perrache, straight ahead for the Riviera, to the left to Grenoble, which is the direction this TGV takes. The Lyon suburbs are soon behind and the TGV then passes under the Lyon TGV bypass line, mentioned ealier, before threading its way through increasingly hilly countryside to end its journey in Grenoble. On arrival direct access is available from the TGV platform onto Grenoble's futuristic light rail (or tram) system, opened in 1987 and extended in 1990.

Grenoble itself is a very pleasant large town and one of the few places I know where the pavements are actually washed, as opposed to just being swept. If you are in the area for a few days some local excursions might include a return trip on a diesel railcar to Veynes (about three trains a day run on this line), a spectacular ride as the line climbs to about 3,000 metres and includes a reverse curve (where the lower line is directly visible from the upper two lines) and stations with notices such as "Lampiserie" (lamp-room) and "Magasin" (station store) above doorways!

Another suggested excursion (for railway enthusiasts in particular) is to take the train to Veynes and alight at St Georges de Commiers. From here a vintage electric (yes, electric!) train climbs about 1,000 metres to La Mure, where you can take in the surrounding scenery (although not far from Grenoble, due to the infrequency of local trains, this excursion takes up the best part of a day).

Grenoble, at the foot of the Alps, is also a good place to start a walking or cycling holiday.

Bordeaux-Paris and Paris-Rennes

by Martin Thorne

The TGV Atlantique (from now on abbreviated TGV-A) started operating in September 1989. This is the second of three high-speed lines to be built (the third is TGV Nord, which links Paris and Brussels with the Channel Tunnel (and, eventually, London) and opened in 1993). The TGV-A was not built as a completely new railway line, as was the line from Paris to Lyon, but basically to increase passenger capacity on railway lines to west and south-west France which were approaching saturation point at the approaches to Paris.

The TGVs used on this new line are a considerable advancement on the original TGV trains used on the Paris-Lyon route. The latest technology has been used to improve passenger comfort and environment (for instance electronic displays showing the next station stop are shown at both ends of each coach, both inside and outside).

The journey from Bordeaux to Paris (Montparnasse) uses part of the old main line and all the new high-speed line to Paris. The fastest journey time is around three hours.

After departing from Bordeaux the TGV crosses the River Gironde before heading out into open countryside towards Tours. The particular TGV I travelled on called at Angoulême and Poitiers. About ten miles outside Tours, the TGV joins the TGV bypass, built to avoid the bottleneck at Tours (which is a terminal station). Speed rapidly builds up to 300 kph (186 mph), the maximum permitted. The River Loire is crossed and the line then enters a 1.5km tunnel, the first of several built on this high-speed line, in view of environmental considerations (it passes under some vine-yards, and rumour has it that the vibrations from the TGVs passing under-neath helps ferment the grapes!).

The line from Tours joins up with the high-speed line about 30 miles north of Tours. The purpose-built station at Vendôme is passed and a few miles further on the high-speed branch from Le Mans joins the main high-speed line. For about 20 miles the high-speed line parallels the local Bretigny-Tours line, which also serves as an emergency access/exit point. After the two lines part company the high-speed line then parallels the A10 motorway and enters a series of tunnels, speed by this time being reduced as the TGV approaches the Paris suburbs. (An outer suburban TGV station, at Massy Palaiseau facilitates an easy interchange between the Paris subur-ban rail network and the TGV.)

On the approach to Paris (Montparnasse) the high-speed line was able to make use of the trackbed of an abandoned suburban railway to bring it to within a mile of Montparnasse. Montparnasse station was itself completely rebuilt for the TGV-A and is an impressive glass and chrome structure on several levels connected by escalators.

The TGV to Rennes retraces the route as far as the high-speed junction just north of Vendôme. This high-speed branch is about 30 miles in length and rejoins the original Paris-Le Mans main line about 15 miles outside Le Mans (a TGV bypass is currently being planned to take the line around Le Mans, another bottleneck).

After a brief call at Le Mans, famous for its 24-hour road race, the TGV travels at a maximum speed of 125 mph through pleasant countryside before reaching the historic town of Rennes. Regrettably, the railway station has been rebuilt to resemble a smaller version of Montparnasse and is totally out of character with the rest of the town. A better job has been made at Morlaix, though, on the recently electrified line to Brest, where the station, near the magnificent viaduct, has been completely refurbished.

Paris-Nantes

by Graham Tolliday

A day trip from Paris to Nantes is perfectly possible, using the superb service of TGV-A trains. For example, at the time of writing, from Paris (Gare Montparnasse) the 0850 reaches Nantes at 1056; the 0950 at 1201. For the return journey, the 1728 reaches Paris non-stop at 1930.

French Railways

The TGV Atlantique passes the village of Mauves on the River Loire

For late risers, even the 1125 from Paris allows four hours in Nantes, ample time for exploration and for sampling the excellent new tramway that crosses the city.

Nantes is one of the most important cities in western France, with a population of about 260,000. It straddles the River Loire at the confluence of the two tributaries, the Sèvre and the Erdre, the latter tunnelled under the city. Although sea-going ships can reach the port of Nantes, St Nazaire is nearby at the mouth of the Loire. The castle, now a tramway stop, was founded in the tenth century, and was the residence of the Dukes of Brittany. The Gothic cathedral was founded in 1434, not completed until the 19th century, and almost destroyed by fire in 1972. It has now been completely restored and is conveniently situated near the railway station.

Directly opposite the station are the Botanical Gardens, among the best the writer has visited, with 400 varieties of camellias, magnolias, and a mass of colour and variety. This is only one of five public parks, including a Japanese-style garden along the banks of the Erdre.

Nantes suffered much destruction in the Second World War, but there are few signs of this today. It was the birthplace of Jules Verne (1828-1905).

Normally the TGVs cruise at a modest 140/150 mph, at which speed the quality of ride is superb — so different from BR's ill-fated APT (Advanced Passenger Train). The Paris-Nantes journey is 240 miles, average speed with stops at Le Mans and Angers 123 mph, but non-stop trains average 140 mph.

Not only are the trains superb, but the SNCF builds special tracks for them which, like the old Roman roads, follow straight lines where gradients pose no problem. Thus far 100 TGV Atlantiques have been built, and 480 are on order. RENFE (Spanish Railways) has built a standard gauge high speed line between Madrid and Seville, and bought its AVE (Alta Velocidad Española), based on the TGV, from GEC-Alsthom, which is also building the Trans-Manche Supertrains, even those, hopefully, to be used north of London. The export potential is enormous.

Some TGV travel tips

Compulsory combined seat reservations and supplements apply to all TGV services (it is known as RESA TGV). These can vary from £2.00 to £8.00 (second class). They can be booked from BR stations (check locally) and from rail appointed travel agents.

If you are unlucky enough to have reserved a seat in the last few coaches of a two-train TGV set, be prepared for a long walk, as they can reach a length of half a kilometre!

Footnotes

Currently under construction and due to open in 1994, is a Paris TGV Bypass. This will enable TGVs from Brussels, London etc to travel direct to the French Riviera and south-western France. Two stations are also being built, at Paris (Roissy) Airport and at EuroDisneyland.

The TGVs currently working on the Paris-Lyon route are to be replaced over the next few years by double-decked TGVs, to increase capacity. They will also be used on the TGV Nord between Paris and Lille, Brussels and, eventually, Amsterdam and Cologne.

CHAPTER 5

Historic French cities

Railtrail 1: Northern France

Northern France is bedecked by a necklace of historic cities, many of which have a distant or more recent historical interest for the British visitor.

The opening of the Channel Tunnel makes it easier to spend a short break in one of them, or to roam between them by train.

Most are served by fast radial routes from Paris. If the Eurostar train has brought you to the Gare du Nord, three hours after leaving Waterloo, you could take one of a number of Métro connections or a direct bus to the Gare St Lazare, terminus of two key routes into Normandy.

Turbotrains from St Lazare operate 15 services a day, with a journey time of just under two hours, to Caen, before continuing to the port of Cherbourg. Bayeux and St Lô can also be reached this way.

Local trains run between Caen and Rouen, taking about two hours for the 100 miles, but the service is not frequent. These trains pass through the riverside town of Elbeuf, south of Rouen, terminus of the ten-mile Chemin de fer Touristique de la Forêt de la Londe. Vintage diesel railcars take you on a scenic run through the forest which contains the ruined castle of

Tree-lined boulevards flank the Bassin St Pierre at Caen, a tranquil scene which belies a nightmare ordeal in June 1944 when 80 per cent of the city was destroyed in bombing raids

Robert le Diable (Robert the Devil) — William the Conqueror's father. The trains only run on Sundays and public holidays. For details, contact the Club Ferroviaire d'Elbeuf, Gare d'Elbeuf Ville, 6500 Elbeuf.

The city of Rouen is on the electrified main line from Paris St Lazare to Le Havre, and enjoys some 18 express trains a day. The fastest takes just one hour eight minutes for the 87 miles.

Amiens is 82 miles from Paris on the classic route to Calais, and just over an hour from the capital. It is also served from the junction of Longueau, on the classic route north to Lille, which also serves Arras, 124 miles from Paris and just over 90 minutes by the fastest trains. Having perhaps sped to Paris from London by TGV, you may prefer to make your way back home in more leisurely fashion via these interesting cities of Normandy and Picardy. The route from Rouen to Amiens is likely to feature in this pilgrimage, and is described by Giles Angell.

ROUEN TO AMIENS : SEINE TO SOMME
by Giles Angell

Rouen is perhaps best known for its association with Joan of Arc.

A bridge over the Seine, named after the Martyr, continues as the rue Jeanne d'Arc to the weather beaten, carved stone façade of Rouen Rive Droite — the surviving passenger station which was rebuilt in its present art nouveau style in 1928.

After passing through a 2km tunnel, the line crosses a viaduct to reveal Rouen Cathedral's spire, easily recognisable to the left as we climb. The line then curves round the eastern suburbs and out into undulating country-side to reach the first village on our journey, St Martin-du-Vivier.

Then, shallow cuttings, arable fields and grazing land alternate along the twin-track as it passes through deciduously wooded valleys. On Morgny's opposite platform, notice the goods shed which has been converted into a tennis court.

Longuerue-Vie-Manoir boasts a dovecot-style granary and weatherboarded chequer-tiled station house in contrast to the concrete "standing stones" which border the station car park. After the junction of Monterolier-Buchy, with its island platform, notice the nearby terraced cottage embellished with ston e— a typical feature of the line.

After another long tunnel, followed by distant views of undulating countryside to the north, the train runs through the forest of Epinay before a brick skewbridge and trailing junction, right, brings us to Serqueux, the only town en route.

You can change here for direct trains to Pontoise and Paris. Cascading, overhanging pilasters, recessed keystones and receding sequence arches over Palladian-style windows, make the station building a study in redbrick.

At Gaillefontaine there are distant views of countryside to the south and just before Formerie the overgrown sidings present a charming scene as does the station building with its iron lacework and shutters.

Creepers covering the goods shed at Abancourt mask the cement works sidings on the left, and freight activity by the trailing junction, right. Espalier trees grace the two island platforms further on. After Abancourt the train passes through scrubland, then Romescamps. At Fouilloy, "station green" larches, characterise an area where church spires resemble concertinaed ice-cream cornets. Beyond Sainte-Segnée the train crosses a viaduct spanning a fertile gorge before reaching Poix de Picardie station with its sycamore trees, then Famechon with its rowans.

Cornerstones enhance the brick portals of the kilometre-long brick tunnel portal and wooden buffers in the long grass blend in well with the rustic surroundings at Namps-Quevauvillers. After passing the disused station of Martello, the grain silos at Saleux and then Pont Demetz, the train accelerates on its way to Saint-Roch (Somme) where gables and mansard roofs crown the impressive station building which overlooks a central island platform.

Sidings widen then narrow as the tracks funnel under retaining walls prior to meeting the line's architectural highlight — an ornate hollow-arched bridge before entering Amiens station — Notice the unusual, curved passenger bridge which contrasts with the stark geometric surroundings.

This restful journey through the Normandy countryside bridges the old with the new: the older world of Rouen, birthplace of Jean of Arc with the more modern world of Amiens, home to Jules Verne (see page 44).

ARRAS

by Trevor Garrod

Arras suffered badly during the First World War and many of the roads which lead to the city across open fields pass small, neat cemeteries containing the remains of those who fell.

Today, the historic city centre has been carefully restored and is one of the places which no discerning visitor to northern France should miss.

From the railway station, which is conveniently situated next to the bus station, cross the Place Maréchal Foch and then the broad boulevard which has been built on the site of the old city walls. Narrow streets then lead you to the city's two great central squares bordered with tall stone and brick houses dating from the 17th and 18th centuries, surmounted by elegant curved Flemish gables, and with cool arcades below. The Grand Place covers two hectares; the Place des Héros, is dominated by the magnificent town hall with its 75-metre high belfry. You can climb the 326 steps to the top or take a lift for most of the way. Inside the town hall are interesting displays of local history.

Arras also has a massive 18th century cathedral and, next to it, the abbey buildings which house the municipal museum in which you can see one of the tapestries which brought the name of this city into the English language. Students of Shakespeare may recall that, in Hamlet, Polonius was stabbed when hiding behind an arras. Incidentally, much of the wool used in these tapestries was imported from England.

Arras was also the home town of two famous men. Maximillian de Robespierre, a local lawyer, was leader of the Jacobins in the French Revolution and presided over the execution of many of the nobility before losing his own head at the guillotine in 1794. He is commemorated by a rue de Robespierre in the old part of the city.

In our own century, Guy Mollet, Mayor of Arras from 1945 to 1975, played a key role in founding the European Community, served for a short time as French Prime Minister, and is credited with the development of the busy, prosperous city we see today.

AMIENS

by Ann Holt

The line from the Channel plunges into a cutting on its approach to this town of some 130,000 inhabitants. Your first sight, on emerging from the station, is the Tour Perret —104 metres high and the work of Auguste Perret, a pioneer in the use of reinforced concrete. Though not likely to be seen by most as a thing of beauty, its "lantern" top makes it more interesting than many later examples of the technique. It was built as part of the post-war reconstruction of Amiens after the 1939-45 war in which 60 per cent of the city was destroyed. The city was also heavily shelled during the 1914-18 war. Luckily Amiens' great glory, the cathedral, survived both.

There are Tourist Information offices in front of the station, the cathedral and at the Maison de la Culture, the latter, unfortunately, on the other side of town.

From the station, take the rue de Noyon, then a right turn into the rue Victor Hugo, which leads, on the right, to the Museum of Local and Regional Art and History. Housed in a 17th century building of pink brick and white stone, the museum includes portraits of two of Amiens' literary personalities — Choderlos de Laclos, a native of the city, whose book *Les Liaisons Dangereuses* scandalised the 18th century and, though rather more staid, Jules Verne, who lived here for most of his life and was town councillor.

At the end of the street is the cathedral and a view of the apse, surrounded by flying buttresses and topped by a slender spire carved at the beginning of the 16th century. Most of the building dates from the 13th century, when Amiens gained great prosperity from the cloth trade. On the south side, the street passes a graceful porch leading to the west front. Although the stone has suffered from the effects of pollution, the three sumptuously decorated portals and, above them, the arcades, unmatched towers and rose window, create a wonderfully rich ensemble. Inside, the carved oak choir stalls are a masterpiece of 16th century flamboyance.

Rue des Luzarches from the south porch leads to the 16th century Logis du Roi and the adjoining Maison de Sagittaire, home of an 18th century philosophical and artistic society known as the Rosati. Nearby, in rue des Trois Cailloux, a bank hides behind a graceful façade, which is all that remains of a theatre built in 1780, another victim of war. The street continues to Place Gambetta, where a turn left on to rue de la République leads to the Musée de Picardie, which has an interesting archeological and fine art collection.

If you are leaving in the direction of Paris, if possible get a seat facing backwards on the left hand side of the train. As the train pulls away from Amiens you will see, rising above the town, the apse and flying buttresses of the cathedral.

ROUEN

by Ann Holt

Rouen is the capital of the department of Haute Normandie, France's fifth port and has some 100,000 inhabitants. It first became a prosperous centre after it was ceded to the Dukes of Normandy in the 10th century and remained economically important until the decline of its industries 800 years later. The Tourist Information office is opposite the cathedral.

From the station there are buses along the rue Jeanne d'Arc. Look out for the rue du Gros Horloge. The "horloge" (clock) in question dates from 1389 and occupies an arch over the street, where it was placed in 1527. Beside it is a tower from the top of which you can get a fine view of the city. The street eventually opens into a "square" in front of the cathedral.

This view of the west front provided the impressionist painter Monet with the subject for a series of canvasses exploring the play of light on the cathedral's elaborately decorated surface. The building dates from the 12th century with later additions providing excellent illustrations of the evolution of the Gothic style. The interior is dominated by soaring columns. At the extreme east end is the chapel of the Virgin, containing an elaborate early 16th century tomb of two cardinals, uncle and nephew, both named Georges d'Amboise.

The old quarter of Rouen is famous for its half-timbered houses and a walk through its streets is highly recommended. Rue St Romain along the north side of the cathedral leads, across rue de la Republique, to the church of St Maclou, a masterpiece of the flamboyant style. To the north on rue Martainville is its charnel house, complete with gruesome decoration.

From the west front of St Maclou, rue Damiette leads to another superb Gothic church, that of St Ouen. Rue de l'Hôpital leads from the Place in front of the church back towards the centre and rue Ganterie. Rue de l'Ecureuil, to the right leads to the Musée des Beaux Arts, which has a notable collection, the church of St Godard, famous for its stained glass, and in the former church of St Laurent, a museum of wrought iron work. Rue de Socrate to the left leads to the 16th century Palais de Justice, much damaged in 1944, but now restored.

Across rue Jeanne d'Arc from the Palais de Justice, rue Rollon leads to the Place du Vieux-Marché where, in May 1431, Jeanne d'Arc was burned at the stake. On the way back to the station, turn off rue Jeanne d'Arc onto rue du Donjon, where a tower remains of the castle in which she was imprisoned. Inside is a museum giving the history of the castle and its most famous prisoner.

CAEN

by Alan Maitland

This completely replanned city of tree-lined boulevards and green spaces and bridges bedecked with floodlit fountains spanning the placid Orne is an impressive example of the French genius for reconstruction. Looking at Caen today, it is hard to believe that 80 per cent of the city was destroyed in June, 1944 during a series of horrific bombing raids. Despite all that destruction the city has gained an attractive, open character, and still has more of interest at its heart than could ever be encompassed in one visit — six medieval churches (one of them, St Pierre, of quite exceptional beauty), two perfect Norman abbeys, an outstanding modern gallery, a unique museum, Memorial pour la Paix, and probably the best shopping to be had in Normandy.

The narrow streets of the old quarter, and the churches of St Pierre and St Jean, have achieved a rebirth so perfect that it's difficult to believe that 50 years ago they were in ruins. (It was a spectacular direct hit from *HMS Rodney* that brought down the tower and spire of St Pierre).

This was William the Conqueror's capital. To settle a difference with the Pope, he and his queen had great churches built within a mile of each other — Matilda her Abbaye-aux-Femmes, and William his Abbaye-aux-Hommes (Abbey of the Laddies, as my guidebook endearingly has it!). Both lie buried in superb Norman abbeys (or at least a thigh bone of William's does: the rest of him disappeared during the Revolution). In St Etienne's magnificent nave, very much like that of Norwich with the great open arches of its triforium, thousands of citizens sought refuge during the apocalyptic nights of bombardment in June,1944.

The postwar restoration of William's castle in the centre of the city was a triumph too, marvellously transforming a pre-war dump into a green jewel of gardens and lawns. Garlands lie on the grave of Caen's "Unknown Citizen", an unidentified victim of the raids. From the ramparts, as the golden lions on Normandy's standard strain into the wind, a panoramic view takes in the towers and spires of this amiable and civilised city.

Turbotrains from St Lazare operate 15 services a day with a journey time just under two hours. Caen station is south of the river and within walking distance of rue St Jean and Avenue du 6 Juin, the two main streets leading to the chateau; or you can take CTAC city buses 1, 3, 11, 12, or 16 to Place Courtonne. The memorial is well outside the centre, on Esplanade Dwight Eisenhower, but served directly by CTAC bus ligne 17. The tourist office is in Place St Pierre, directly opposite to where the doors of Caen's beloved St Pierre stand wide open in welcome. It should not be missed.

Further Explorations of Normandy from Gare St Lazare or from Caen

One stop beyond Bayeux, deep in rural Normandy, is the country junction marked by IGN on its maps simply as "Gare de Lison". You change here for Coutances, a charming old hill-top city whose cathedral spires can be seen miles away — and St Lô, heroic city of the Battle of Normandy. Despite the smart new unit of Train Express Régional (TER) Basse-Normandie standing in the bay, however, the journey is more than likely to be made under SNCF's 'bustitution' policy for this under-used line.

St Lô was virtually annihilated in 1944 but its heroism was recognised with the award of the Croix de Guerre and the Légion d'Honneur which have now been incorporated into the city coat-of-arms.

The city is entirely new in appearance, though the ramparts of the walls built in Charlemagne's time have been restored. On their heights, overlooking the river, the tragically shattered West Front of St Lô's beautiful Notre Dame is pulled together by a starkly sombre plain wall that is a sermon in itself on the futility of war.

Also worth a visit is Haras du St Lô, part of the National Stud, where you can see some beautiful equine specimens including the magnificent Norman Percherons; open every day from mid-July.

Railtrail 2: Eastern France

While historic towns and cities of northern France often have links with Britain, those of eastern France testify more to the relations over the centuries between the French and their eastern neighbours, the Germans. Indeed, Alsace-Lorraine, with the cities of Metz, Strasbourg and Mulhouse was, before the First World War, and therefore still within living memory, part of the German Empire.

These places can all be reached from the Gare de l'Est in Paris, just a couple of streets away from the Gare du Nord; or, in most cases, by cross-country services from Lille.

The trunk route strikes out eastwards across Champagne to Nancy and Strasbourg, with an important branch leaving it at Epernay for Rheims and Charleville-Mézières. Rheims, the capital of the Champagne region, is itself just north of the wine-producing area, 173 km from Paris and reached, in

Among the many exhibits at the SNCF museum at Mulhouse in southern Alsace are coaches once used on the Orient Express and the Imperial saloon of Napoleon III

just over 1 $^{1}/_{2}$ hours, by the fastest trains. Some of these work through to Charleville-Mezières or Longwy and connect with trains on the Lille-Metz cross-country route.

Nancy is 353km from Paris and the distance can be covered in 2 hours 40 minutes. Often Nancy is the first stop for expresses to Strasbourg, 151km further on and some four hours from the capital. For Metz, you can take the Paris-Luxembourg service which runs at approximately two-hourly intervals.

Strasbourg, Colmar, Mulhouse and other towns of Alsace are also served by frequent local and long-distance trains. Often local services in this region, and elsewhere, are partly maintained by the regional government and decked out in a distinctive livery.

If you want to wander at a more leisurely pace around eastern France, look carefully at the timetable and you will find some cross-country services such as Lille-Rheims and Lille-Metz. Alternatively, you can wander down from Brussels via Luxembourg to Metz and Nancy; or even make a trip into this region after exploring the German Mosel, perhaps using the occasional local trains that hug the bank of the river, below the vine-clad slopes, from Trier down to Thionville. Those in search of something different may also take the local train between Metz and Thionville and alight at Big-Bang Schtroumpf — the new station serving the theme park of that name, built on the site of a former steelworks. These days, there is little trouble in crossing and recrossing the borders; you can simply use Cooks' International Timetable from which to mix the ingredients for a tour of a region which has had more than its share of upheavals in the past but can now, with some justification, call itself truly European.

RHEIMS

by Trevor Garrod

Rheims has been an important city for over 2,000 years, and in Roman times had as many as 80,000 inhabitants. Today's figure is about twice that number. Nine main roads, many of Roman origin, converge on the capital of Champagne from all directions. It is not on the main railway from Paris to the east, but is served by the important electrified route branching off at Epernay for Charleville, the cross-country line from Amiens to Châlons-sur-Marne, and a secondary route from Trilport, also on the main line.

The tourist office is conveniently situated on the square in front of the spacious well-appointed station. From here, it is an easy walk across a leafy square bordered by two boulevards to the Place Drouet d'Erlon, an elegant pedestrianised street leading into the heart of the ancient city. If you continue into the rue des Capucins, to where it crosses the rue Libergier, your eye will be taken by the great western façade of the cathedral.

This grand edifice, adorned by pinnacles and statues, was built in a relatively short time in the 13th century, its two towers being completed in 1480. You can admire the light, harmonious interior, 150 metres in length, before wandering outside and, perhaps, visiting the museum in the 16th century Archbishop's Palace on the south side. It was in this cathedral that most French kings were crowned.

A walk southwards down the rue Voltaire and rue Gambetta brings you to the Basilica of St Remi, the sixth century martyr who gave the city its modern name. Originally part of a mediaeval abbey, it has been tastefully restored this century.

Even if you were not aware of the regal and other historical associations of Rheims, you will doubtless have associated sparkling wine with the region of which it is capital; and close to the basilica are the "caves de Champagne" — subterranean galleries where, on working days, you can see how it is made.

If you have more time to spend in this interesting city, there is the large Parc Pommery with its swimming pool, children's playground and sports facilities to visit as well as the modern Maison de la Culture with its exhibition halls and fine mediaeval and Renaissance buildings to see around the city hall.

Finally, if it is principally the wine that has drawn you to Champagne, you will find, a few miles south of the city, the Montagne de Rheims, a forested ridge up to 287 metres high, with vineyards on its slopes. The rail line from Rheims to Epernay passes through it, and under it by the $3 \ ^1/_2$km tunnel of Rilly-la-Montagne. The small town of that name, with its own station, is worth a visit for its church, vineyards and walks in the hills which give fine views of Rheims on the plain below.

VERDUN

by Trevor Garrod

You reach Verdun by leaving the main line train from Paris at Châlons-sur-Marne, or less frequently from Metz, and taking a diesel train through quiet countryside. The town occupies both banks of the Meuse — here a small, placid river — fringed by a wooded ridge to the east and gently undulating farmland to the west.

As you leave the station and walk along the Avenue Garibaldi, however, a foretaste of this small town's long history looms to your right in the form of the Porte St Paul (St Paul's Gate)— one of the last vestiges of the fortifications that surrounded it until 1919.

Turn right and you reach the great stone Victory Monument at the top of a flight of steps. It is dedicated to "ceux de Verdun" ("those of Verdun") and its crypt contains the golden books commemorating the thousands of men and women decorated for their part in the savage battles that raged around this small but strategic town in 1916.

Over the centuries, Verdun has had more than its share of war and the names of many of the streets and squares remind you of this, as does the massive 14th century Porte Chaussée, one street away, guarding the oldest bridge across the river.

A short stroll up through narrow streets brings you to the cathedral, cloisters and bishop's palace which, between them, show a blend of styles from the early middle ages to the 18th century. Then, a few paces further on, you are back in the theatre of war with the massive citadel whose underground rooms and passages sheltered some 2,000 French soldiers during the First World War. There is still a military presence here, but you can also visit an impressive museum in the citadel.

When Verdun was under siege in 1916, there was only one road into the town: the Voie Sacrée, or Sacred Way, from the south-west. Fighting went on all around and perhaps the most moving way to appreciate the scale of it is to walk or cycle up into the woods to the north-east or take a coach organised by the tourist office.

As you enter the trees, signs in three languages warn against picnics, playing games or music. This is a place of pilgrimage, dedicated to all those who died. You pass the monument to André Maginot, Local Deputy and architect of the Maginot Line of 1930s fortifications. Further up is a museum which depicts what warfare was like in the then bleak wilderness of these uplands in which nine villages had been wiped off the map, in 1916. The culmination of your pilgrimage is the smooth, stark, white tower and the long, white chamber of the Ossuaire de Douaumont, at the highest point, overlooking immaculate lawns. Its marble tombs contain the remains of tens of thousands of dead. Like the museum, it has to be entered in silence.

Today's Verdun is a pleasant and peaceful place, where you can relax in the riverside park and contemplate its symbol — a large "V" formed by two arms and two hands crossed in friendship. Your visit will not be easily forgotten.

NANCY

by Trevor Garrod

The city of Nancy, situated in the valley of the Meurthe and surrounded by wooded hills, is the capital of Lorraine and one of the most attractive cities of eastern France.

The station is on the edge of the "new town", dating from the 17th and 18th centuries, its streets forming a dignified rectilinear pattern. A walk along the main rue Stanislas or its parallel rue Poincaré brings you to Nancy's architectural gem: the Place Stanislas. This great square measures 124 metres by 106 and is surrounded on three sides by imposing 18th century buildings, the largest of them the City Hall. Pavilions and a triumphal arch on the fourth side take the eye through to the Place de la

Carrière, with its rows of trees and its fountains. At the entrances and corners of the Place Stanislas are wrought-iron gateways and railings, their intricacies picked out in gold leaf, while the centre is dominated by a statue of Stanislas, King of Poland, whose design it was.

As you take a leisurely coffee at one of the terraces facing the square, and drink in the scene, you may wonder how Stanislas King of Poland came to this very French city. As father-in-law of Louis XV, and dethroned in his own country, he was given the then vacant Duchy of Lorraine and spent the next 30 years embellishing and enhancing his new capital city.

When you are ready, stroll through the Place de la Carrière, where 18th century Frenchmen exercised their horses, and turn left into the narrow streets of the medieval city. Places to visit here include the 13th century Palace of the Dukes, the Museum of Lorraine's history and, at the northern end of the Grande-Rue, a gateway of the original walled city which for many years served as a prison.

From here, a short walk through a back street brings you into the large park of La Pépinière, with its zoo. Then, if your stay in Nancy is to be a longer one, there are churches, museums, art galleries and an 18th century cathedral to be explored.

Nancy is just over two and a half hours from Paris by the fastest trains, and also enjoys a frequent service to neighbouring Metz via Pont-à-Mousson with its impressive riverside abbey. If you are travelling on to Strasbourg, and have time, catch a train that stops at Lunéville, with its chateau, or Saverne, a small attractively situated town among woods and vineyards at the foot of the Vosges.

METZ

by Michael Oakley

When planning the East main line from Paris the 19th century railway builders had an obvious destination in Strasbourg. This major city of the East has always been a natural transport interchange, surrounded by the water of the Rhine and Ill rivers and the Rhine-Marne and Rhine-Rhône canals. It is considered to be France's fifth largest port, in spite of being so far inland.

What may have been a bit harder was the route through the hills at the northern end of the Vosges range. In particular, the twin cities of Metz and Nancy, lying directly north-south only 50km apart, made for a difficult choice. Metz would have offered easier terrain, but in the event Nancy was held the more important of the two. The ironic result is that Nancy has remained the major stop between Paris and Strasbourg but not much else, while Metz has become the focus for a much wider range of services on secondary and cross-country main lines.

SNCF express on the Metz to Strasbourg line

Little clues to the turbulent history of this region can be found on its railways even today. The Alsace-Lorraine region was changing hands as a political pawn long before becoming the focus of Franco-German conflict. More immediately obvious is that right-hand running is the rule on the railways throughout the area, instead of left which applies on most of SNCF. This was probably the German influence in the main, though it is, of course, Napoleon who is credited with trying to make everyone keep right instead of left — and with being more successful with those he conquered than those at home! Substantial flyovers enable the change from left to right to be made as trains approach the area, to the west of Sarrebourg, Metz and Hayange.

Another clue to how the system developed is the lineside kilometre-posting, mostly on the north and east side of lines in the area. Paris to Strasbourg is measured straight through via Nancy, but the branch from Reding to Metz takes up a measure from zero at Strasbourg and continues with it to the border of Luxembourg.

Metz nowadays considers itself a more "modern" city than Nancy. It has retained the narrow old town where Rabelais was the physician in the 16th century, and the archly Gothic cathedral with its renowned stained glass can be seen rearing above the buildings on the banks of the Moselle. However, the urban sprawl now surrounds everything.

Known as "La cité aux vingt-deux ponts" (city with 22 bridges), Metz needed many bridges as the Moselle splits into several channels here and is also joined by the River Seille. It was founded by the Romans and its ancient monuments include the church of St-Pierre-aux-Nonnains, built between the fourth and seventh centuries, and the 13th century Porte des Allemands. The principal trains from Paris take off by a secondary route from the east main line at Lérouville, climbing gently over a belt of low rolling hills and open farmland. The small town of Onville retains a few express calls, but even SNCF has given up on most of the other villages en route. Metz station itself is large and depressing, having been rebuilt partly under a concrete raft. Here services split for Germany and Luxembourg.

STRASBOURG
by Trevor Garrod

The city of Strasbourg has, at stages in its 2,000-year history, held great significance for both France and Germany. It has always been an international crossroads and indeed its very name is said to derive from Strateburgum — "the town where roads meet".

Leading German figures like Gutenberg the printer, and Goethe the poet and dramatist, have lived and worked here; while it was in this city, in 1792, that Rouget de Lisle composed the French national anthem, *La Marseillaise*, and Jean-Pierre Clause first produced pâté de foie gras. Since 1949, Strasbourg has been the seat of the Council of Europe.

Arriving by train in Strasbourg's clean, imposing station, you may proceed via modern shop-lined subways into the rue du Faubourg National, soon crossing one of the branches of the River Ill. The old part of the city is built on an island and many pleasant hours can be spent strolling through its narrow streets, eating and drinking at open-air cafés and sampling the full range of shops that you would expect to find in a city of a quarter of a million people.

Not to be missed are La Petite France and the great cathedral of Notre Dame. The former is a picturesque waterside quarter of wooden houses, dating from the 16th century, and ancient ramparts. Notre Dame, built in stages from the 12th to the 15th centuries, is a splendid example of Gothic architecture, characterised by its massive west front and twin towers, of which the northern one is surmounted by a detailed and delicate spire.

Inside the cathedral is another masterpiece: the astrological clock which is set through all its intricate motions at 12.30 each day.

When you have had your fill of the old city, with its nine museums, many churches and interesting byways, you can take a walk or boat trip northwards, past elegant 19th century boulevards, to the Palace of Europe, opened in 1977 on the lush green banks of the Ill. This imposing white building, the flags of 12 nations fluttering before it, is open to the public at certain times. The 518 MEPs usually also meet in public here for one week each month, their deliberations interpreted simultaneously into the nine official languages of the European Community.

MEPs and their staff tend to lead a jet-setting life, commuting between their constituencies and their places of work in Strasbourg, Luxembourg and Brussels. Fast trains will also get you there from these two capitals and also from Paris Est, which is just under four hours away by the fastest trains.

MULHOUSE AND SOUTHERN ALSACE

by Tony Smale

Why did the French railway company, SNCF, decide on a small, industrial town in the eastern corner of the country for its national railway museum? Perhaps they had seen an illustration dating from around 1550 showing the use of rail-guided waggons in the local silver mines, some 200 years before the advent of mineral railways in the north-east of England. Certainly, there was a railway line in Alsace as early as 1839. Europe's first international rail route passed here a few years later. The museum owes its existence as much to the aspirations of the Industrial Society of Mulhouse as to SNCF's desire for a suitable, permanent home for its growing collection.

Mulhouse had long been associated with the building of locomotives. In order to continue this tradition after the loss of Alsace-Lorraine to the Germans in 1871, the SACM company (Société Alsacienne de Construction Méchanique) was set up in the neighbouring territory of Belfort, which remained part of France. The railways of Alsace-Lorraine were "Prussianised" and converted to right-hand running before the territory was regained under the Treaty of Versailles in 1919. As the premier works of the Alsthom company (now GEC Alsthom), the Belfort factory continues to play a major rôle in the railway industry with the construction of the record-breaking TGV trains.

The national railway collection was temporarily located in the disused depot of Mulhouse-Nord in 1971, then moved to the present museum site in June 1976. Most of the collection is displayed in the main exhibition hall, which has nearly a mile of track arranged in 12 parallel bays. There are further exhibits in an open-air yard, and beyond that is the museum's own station on the mainline to Strasbourg (although used only for special group visits).

Among the colourful parade of coaches on display are grand Pullman cars of the Orient Express and Golden Arrow, the Imperial saloon of Napoleon III and the presidential coach used by de Gaulle. The carriages of the Grand Duchess of Luxembourg are a reminder of the period when Luxembourg's railways were operated by the Alsace-Lorraine administration. Delightfully eccentric vehicles are plentiful, for example, a wooden-bodied coach with fresh-air accommodation on the upper deck and a Micheline railcar with eight rubber-tyred wheels per bogie. My particular favourite is a pre-war electric suburban coach, built like a battleship from the steel plates and rivets, and with interior brass fittings and etched glass panels. I remember travelling on just such a vehicle out of Paris Invalides shortly before conversion of the line to RER route C.

For steam enthusiasts, there are all manner of machines from narrow-gauge engines to huge Pacific locomotives: examples from the Nord, Midi and PLM (Paris-Lyon-Mediterranée) companies; designs showing marked British or German influence; examples of the work of famous French engineers such as Alfred de Glehn and André Chapelon. There is even a cut-away locomotive to show you how *la vapeur* was produced. In France, coal was never the cheap, plentiful commodity it was in Britain — the profusion of external pipework and valve gear on a French locomotive is evidence of a concern to design for maximum engine efficiency.

The museum yard is given over to exhibits from the Lines and Buildings Department. Here you can stumble over interesting examples of trackwork, puzzle out the meaning of strange signalling devices and peer into the window of a gatekeepers's cottage. A retired SNCF inspector, whom I had met on the bus from town, cornered me by the vast exhibition of railway sleepers and explained all the various methods of preserving and date-tagging in great detail. Much was lost to the wind due to my imperfect grasp of the language; suffice to say, *les traverses* do not just grow on trees!

The Musée Français du Chemin de Fer is located at 2, rue Alfred de Glehn and can be reached by bus number 17 from Mulhouse Station (S17 on Sundays). It is open from 9am daily except December 25 and 26 and January 1. The admission ticket includes entry to the neighbouring Musée du Sapeur-Pompier (Fire Service).

The industrial town of Mulhouse may not be in the First Division of holiday resorts. Yet it forms an ideal centre for rail excursions and it does manage to keep its industrial base at arm's length, well away from the town centre. A walk into town from the station reveals a number of interesting buildings: a tower remaining from the ancient fortifications; a tall mast topped by a revolutionary restaurant; a Renaissance town hall in the delightful main square. Also worth visiting is the Automobile Museum in the Avenue de Colmar, which boasts around 500 vehicles, some very rare.

Easily reached by train from Mulhouse is the medieval town of Colmar with its pleasant, canal-side walks and the world-famous Unterlinden art collection. On summer weekends, you can take a steam train ride along the west bank of the Rhine from Vogelsheim (near Colmar), then return by boat; unfortunately, buses run to Vogelsheim only once or twice a day.

The Swiss city of Basle is only 20 miles to the south of Mulhouse, and stands astride the Rhine like a fortress at the southern end of the Franco-German frontier. The SNCF station forms a French "customs island" adjacent to the Swiss station, itself one of the main railway hubs of Europe. Here, coaches from a dozen state rail administrations wait in a mixed formation before departing to their home territories: Belgium and Denmark, Austria and Italy, Poland and Russia. The street tramways in Basle have long been a model for other European cities and have received visits from several delegations of British transport planners in recent years.

As a contrast from exploring towns and cities, you can escape into the

Vosges mountains using the network of local rail services in Alsace. The one-hour train journey from Mulhouse to Kruth makes a pleasant afternoon trip. For the first few miles, you can pass extensive potash sidings of the Rhône-Poulenc chemical company. The line then follows the Thur valley through St Amarin and Oderen before coming to an abrupt end at a lone platform just short of Kruth. If you walk up through the village and a little way further, you will come to a fine reservoir set in a steep, wooded valley. Alternatively, take a one-day tour of Vosges, changing trains at Sélestat, St Dié and Nancy. Return to Mulhouse through Épinal, Lure and Belfort.

In Alsace, there are times when the language, the architecture or the cuisine give you a fleeting sense of being in Germany. This is Europe's heartland where cultures flow across frontiers as effortlessly as the international trains every day.

Railtrail 3: Western France

You can speed west or southwards from Paris by TGV and be in Brittany or the Dordogne in a remarkably short time. But also within easy reach of the capital are historic towns and cities on the classic routes, forming a circular trail, which we shall follow anticlockwise.

Versailles is to Paris what Windsor is to London. Like Windsor, it has more than one route from the capital. A suburban train will take you to either the Rive Droite or Rive Gauche terminus; or you can travel from Paris Montparnasse to Versailles Chantiers by either suburban train or one of the long distance services to Granville or Le Mans, and it is from this station, the only through one at Versailles, that your journey westward must be made.

Chartres, whose cathedral is famed well beyond the borders of France, is just over 50 miles from Paris. It is also served by Le Mans trains and occasionally those to Rennes, for it is on what was the main line to Brittany before the Ligne à Grande Vitesse was built.

Beyond Chartres, trains speed at a mile or minute, or faster, through the rolling cornfields of Beauce, to reach Le Mans, famous for its 24-hour car race but with a 2000 year history and a fine Gothic cathedral. Here you have to interchange with TGVs and with cross-country diesel services from Caen to Tours; though with only four or five daily workings, and times sometimes varying, according to the day of the week, you may need to plan this stage of your journey carefully.

The trip along the Loire Valley to Blois and Orléans and then back to Paris is again by electric train, with a more frequent service. Another variation on this trail would be to take a mainline train from Le Mans to Angers, with its massive castle, and then a local or a Nantes-Lyon cross-country service from here to Tours.

VERSAILLES

by Trevor Garrod

King Louis XIII needed to escape from the pressures of 17th century life in Paris, and so in 1624 he had a hunting lodge built at Versailles, 11 miles south-west of the capital. His son Louis XIV spent 100 million francs over a 50-year period reconstructing the lodge into an enormous palace, which became a symbol for the glories of France in the era of the Sun King, 1643-1715, when a series of military conquests abroad was coupled with encouragement of the arts at home.

If you are just making a day trip from Paris, the easiest option is to board an RER train at one of the Left Bank stations. From the Gare d'Austerlitz to the Champs de Mars, the train proceeds in tunnels or cuttings with only fleeting glimpses of daylight. It also calls at the Musée d'Orsay, which is bound to be on the itinerary of the discerning visitor. Then the journey continues in the open air alongside the river to Issy before climbing into wooded hills that have the air of a French Surrey. You enjoy brief views across the Bois de Boulogne and the great meander of the Seine before the train veers southwards through Meudon-Val Fleury and the one-and-a- half-mile long Meudon Tunnel. It emerges to run through more leafy suburbs, calling at three more stations, before reaching the small modernised terminus of Versailles Rive Gauche. From here, it is a stone's throw to the grandiose Hôtel de Ville, where you turn left into the broad central boulevard, and ahead of you is the long facade of the château, dominating a wide cobbled square with, in its centre, a statue of Louis XIV on horseback.

The alternative, right bank, rail route starts from Paris St Lazare, running through industrial districts then calling at a station below La Défense, before proceeding via St Cloud and other fashionable suburbs to Versailles Rive Droite, a small handsome terminus that blends in well with the dignified architecture of the town centre, but is a slightly longer walk from the palace than Rive Gauche.

The Palace of Versailles has played a role not only in French but also in European history. It was here in 1871 that the new German Empire was proclaimed by Bismarck's victorious Prussian troops; and here that the peace treaty was formulated to end the First World War. The great Hall of Mirrors is one of the historic rooms that you will no doubt wish to see.

Beyond the Palace is a vast park, in which you could spend all day. Laid out with classical symmetry, it has flower gardens, a central grand canal in the form of a cross, and woodlands on either side. It is a popular excursion point for families on Sunday afternoons when the fountains are playing; though if you like to imagine yourself as Louis XIV, inspecting his pride and joy, you will probably choose a less busy time.

The bicycle had not yet been invented in the time of the Sun King, and he might well have considered it beneath his dignity to be seen on one — but nowadays you can hire one and explore the estate. There is also boating on the artificial waterway and, for the less energetic, a little motor-train will take you round the grounds.

In a far corner of the park is the hamlet of Trianon with its pavilions, in one of which resided in the 18th century Queen Marie "Let them eat cake" Antoinette. You too can eat cake at one of the small cafés secluded in the woods, and the hectic life of 20th century Paris will seem a world away.

VAL DE SEINE
by Tony Smale

The following is an enjoyable, somewhat circuitous rail tour which can be tacked on to your arrival in Paris from a Normandy port, or to an excursion to Versailles.

Starting from the impressive concourse of Gare St Lazare, head for the Versailles platforms and take the first suburban train stopping at Puteaux. Once beyond the station yards, the train crosses the Seine where it curves north-east towards the sea. Dominating the skyline to the left is the modern business quarter of La Défense; you will arrive there in a few moments.

Alight at Puteaux and proceed to the bay platform where used to wait a rather down-at-heel electric unit, ready to depart on an isolated relic of a once-extensive third-rail electrified network. The route was closed in 1993 for conversion to a modern light-rail system, due to open in 1995.

Immediately on leaving Puteaux, you will be rewarded with a spectacular panorama of the city — the Eiffel Tower rising beyond the Bois de Boulogne and the river in the foreground. The line descends through well-to-do suburbs edging ever closer to the Seine. From Pont de St Cloud onwards, the train hugs the left bank. Once past Pont de Sèvres, there appears to be a massive riverboat floating offshore — this is not a riverboat at all, but Renault's Billancourt factory, closed in the spring of 1992.

Three more stops, then you arrive at the improbable terminus platform at Issy-Plaine. From here, the line used to proceed to Les Invalides, the former terminus for the Région de l'Ouest. Climb a few steps to the high level platform and you will see that the route now forms part of RER line C. You can travel onwards, in a tunnel, to the heart of the city or take the westbound RER train to Versailles Rive Gauche for your visit to the palace (return to St Lazare from Versailles Rive Droite).

CHARTRES
by Richard Pill

Chartres is a splendid place for all people to visit, as they do in their thousands every year and have been doing for over eight centuries.

The history of Chartres stretches back to Roman times, its growth and development intertwined with the rise and spread of Christianity and Christendom. The cathedral of Chartres brings the two together, expounded in its expertly crafted 12th century stained glass windows which portray Biblical stories through contemporary figures and pictures. The windows offer unusual insights into the life of mediaeval Man and his world as well as illustrating the Bible and its messages, with Christ at the centre.

The Cathedral School of Chartres was famed as a place of learning, and the scholar Abélard is said to have worked there. He pioneered the use of dialectic as a method of tackling Theology, using reasoning and questioning rather than simple recitation of a text.

On arrival by train you see the town set before you; and a short walk straight ahead to the Place Châtelet is followed by a short climb up narrow streets to the cathedral. On the left is an impressive gift shop that even sells suits of armour! Perhaps you can think of occasions when you would need one... Nearby is a museum whose exterior 12th century stonework is worth a look. There is also an abundance of church cats on the prowl.

To the rear of the cathedral, whose asymmetrical twin spires dominate the town, are memorial gardens from which you have an excellent view across the valley. From here a town trail (*circuit touristique*) leads you to the old quarter with timbered mediaeval buildings, cobbled streets and a lovely narrow river with friendly ducks eager to have your sandwiches! Restaurants catering for all tastes may also be found here, as you proceed via narrow stone bridges and river walkways ending in a civic park.

If you retrace your steps to the station and turn southwards, you enter the modern part of Chartres, with a Town Hall and comprehensive shopping centre somewhat reminiscent of Canterbury. There is a pleasant pedestrianised area which is a peaceful place for a drink and contemplation.

Back at the station, there is much rail activity to be seen, with well-loaded freight trains 24 hours a day and a network of sidings and carriage cleaning facilities. Three freight-only branches leave the main line here, as does the local passenger route to Courtalain. Outside the station, turn right and right again, over the main line, from where good views may be had. To the left is an arts centre where concerts and displays are held. If you turn left just past here and follow the road for about half a mile you reach a park and, just beyond it, a swimming pool and leisure complex.

For details of eating places and accommodation in Chartres, contact the Office de Tourisme, Place de la Cathédrale, BP 289, F28005 Chartres.

Lastly, Chartres has certain things in common with my home town of Bedford. For example, between 4.30 and 6.00pm the whole station comes alive with hundreds of commuters and the roads full of roaring cars and buses, especially on Fridays when city people are heading for the countryside.

Chartres really does offer something for everyone; but for me the cathedral, and its relationship to the place and its people, brings new meaning to Psalm 81: that if you do your duty to God, he will look after your needs also.

TOURS

by Giles Angell

Emerging from the double-span station of this major city of the Loire Valley, turn round and admire the façade of this imposing building. Figures from female mythology crown each of the four stone columns carrying a city name in bold relief. They survey the square that houses the TGV conference centre, opened in 1993. Care has been taken to harmonise its design with the surrounding buildings such as the Grand Hotel.

Across the square, the Boulevard Heurteloup leads toward the city centre. Wednesday is the best time to visit, when there is a flower market along the central reservation footpath of its westward extension, the Boulevard Béranger. Notice the four stone-carved stalwarts who carry the weight of the balcony of the classically adorned Town Hall.

The town hall, like so many buildings in Tours, exudes civic pride

Department stores line the north side of the rue Nationale, as it leads from the Place Jean-Jaurès down to the river. If you resist the temptation to window-shop, you will reach Pont Wilson within ten minutes. Floods destroyed four arches of the bridge in 1978. These have been skilfully rebuilt to blend with the original 18th century structure.

The Loire invites riverside walks. Upstream a comfortable stroll brings you to Pont de Fils. This pedestrian/cyclist bridge was closed, not by floods, but by the vandalism of a lorrydriver (in 1991) when he tried to cross it for a bet.

Nearby, is the medieval cathedral of St Gatien with its rose window. The magnetism of Bishop Martin, its founder, made Tours a notable place of pilgrimage. The stained-glass window in the apse depicts St Patrick having his heart excised before shipment of the rest of his mortal remains for Irish burial!

There are several attractions nearby. Tours lends itself to the simple pleasure of watching the world go by, and the garden of the Musée des Beaux Arts is ideal for this. Here you will also share the company of a permanent resident who enjoys protected status! In 1904 a circus elephant called Fritz was tormented by a cigarette placed in his trunk. He was so upset by this cruel prank he, alas, had to be put down. Mounted, and wearing successive coats of hide preservative, he has remained in the garden — nowadays protected by a glass case — and much to the fascination of admiring children.

Some of the city's numerous museums are housed in the adjacent Château Royal de Tours: they include the waxworks and the Musée Grevins which depicts the city's royal connection with nearby Amboise through an atmospheric series of 31 tableaux.

Archaeological excavations are taking place off the nearby rue Nationale. Fortunately, civic awareness has meant that much of the charm of the old quarter has been preserved with sympathetic infill complementing the delightful, narrow, irregular, half-timbered streets. These converge on the Place Plumereau where pavement cafés provide a perfect place from which to sit and watch the street theatre — and sample the pleasant ambience of Tours.

Just over an hour from Paris Montparnasse by TGV, or just over two hours from Paris Austerlitz by more conventional train, Tours can form a base for leisurely travel in the true French spirit — by train, bus or bicycle to Azay-le-Rideau, Villandry, Chenonceau, Loches and Amboise among the chateaux in the valleys of the Loire and the Cher. The Tourist Office is in the Boulevard Heurteloup, Tel: 47.05.58.08.

ORLÉANS

by Ann Holt

Orléans was already a centre of population when the Romans added Gaul to their empire and it became a prosperous medieval trading town. The town remains economically important and has some 103,000 inhabitants. It was here that Jeanne d'Arc first confronted the English armies in 1429.

Main line trains stop at Les Aubrais, where passengers for Orléans take a shuttle train. There is a Tourist Information office in front of the station and from it the rue de la République runs down to the town's focal point, a square called the Place du Martroi focussed around a statue of Jeanne d'Arc on horseback, erected in 1855. On the south side is the Pavillon de la

Chancellerie, a classical building of 1759. The rue Royale, a graceful arcaded street which leads down to the river, was built a few years earlier.

Returning up the rue Royale from the bridge over the Loire, the rue du Tambour on the left leads to a charming 16th century house which houses a museum devoted to the writer Charles Péguy. Recrossing the rue Royale leads you to rue de Bourgogne which formed the principle east-west axis of the Gallo-Roman city and retains several notable buildings, including a 17th century convent. This now houses the Prefecture. Opposite, in the rue Pothier, is the 15th century library of the medieval university which made Orléans an intellectual centre. Calvin was one of its students.

Rue Pothier leads to the cathedral of Sainte Croix. Building began in the 13th century and continued until the 16th, but in 1568 severe damage was done by extreme Protestants in the course of the wars of religion. Later restoration retained the Gothic style and the result is somewhat odd, more impressive from a distance than close to. Inside, the choir is decorated with some fine 18th century wood carvings. There is a good view of the apse, with its pinnacles and flying buttresses, from the pleasant garden of the former bishop's palace.

On the north side of the cathedral square is the Musée des Beaux-Arts, which has a comprehensive collection and nearby is the Hôtel Groslot, a Renaissance house in origin though much altered and added to in the 19th century. It is now the Hôtel de Ville (town hall).

Rue Jeanne d'Arc begins at the west front of the cathedral and from it rue Sainte Catherine, on the left, leads to the historic museum, a 16th century building which contains important Gallo-Roman statues. At the end of the rue Jeanne d'Arc is Place Général de Gaulle, where the house in which Jeanne is said to have stayed has been lovingly reconstructed after wartime damage. Place Général de Gaulle is linked to Place du Martroi, from which runs rue de la République, back to the station.

The great Gothic cathedral of Notre Dame, Paris, built between 1163 and 1257

Above: The maritime museum, Amsterdam is just one of the many attractions in this vibrant city
Top: Chateau de Chenonceau spanning the River Cher, near Tours

Cologne cathedral, city landmark and, at 520ft, one of the highest cathedrals in the world

A local train at St Goar on the way to Koblenz

River traffic passes by the Lorelei rock on the Rhine

Cologne trams are among the most efficient in Europe and provide the perfect vehicle for advertising

PART TWO

BENELUX

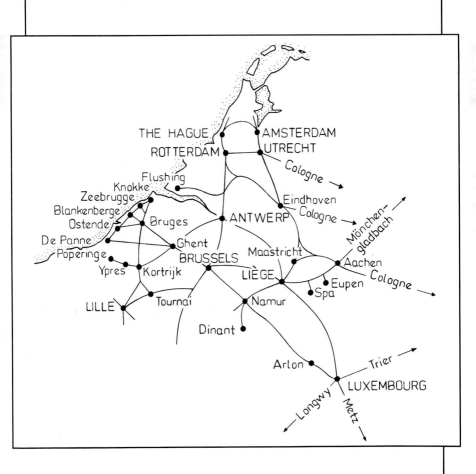

CHAPTER 6

Belgian railtrail

Rails along the coast
by Trevor Garrod

The Belgians have only 40 miles of coastline, but they make the most of it. A string of resorts has grown up along what was originally a line of dunes bordered by sandy beaches and breached by the occasional small harbour. Often the resorts are characterised by lofty close-packed apartment blocks and hotels, built as though the aim was to afford as many residents as possible a view across the ocean. The architecture of these places is not particularly beautiful — but there are also stretches with more attractive and interesting-looking villas among the remaining natural dunes and trees.

The average British seeker of sea, sun and sand may prefer his or her favourite British resort, or to travel to the Mediterranean for a better prospect of sunshine. Yet, for the curious traveller in search of something different, and perhaps touring the ancient cities of Flanders, the Belgian coast is well worth a visit — for what might be termed an "experience".

The coast is easy to reach. Electrified railways branch out from Bruges to Knokke, Zeebrugge and Blankenberge, while the main line from Brussels continues across the flatland to Ostend. The western part of the coast is served by a line from Ghent to Adinkerke-De Panne. Once you are on the coast, travel between the resorts is easy, because all the way from Knokke in the east to De Panne in the west runs a metre-gauge tramway with services every 30 minutes throughout the day. Line 1 trams operate from Knokke to Ostend; line 2 from Ostend to De Panne. The tramway dates from 1886.

Knokke has for over 100 years been a fashionable and gracious resort, famous for its casino and the Zwin nature reserve between the town and the Dutch border. You can also explore its old fishing quarter before taking the tram two miles along the coast to Heist, a smaller but equally pleasant villa resort.

The surroundings change as you reach the growing port of Zeebrugge — literally "Bruges on sea" — founded in 1907 to handle ships that could not reach the ancient inland city. Cargo boats, passenger ferries and fishing vessels are much in evidence. The town itself does not have a lot of attractions, though the tram passes a compact resort area at the western end before speeding out past dunes, parallel to a dual carriageway.

Two miles ahead looms Blankenberge, a typical Belgian resort whose architecture, like its name, is not practically pretty. However, it is a very popular destination for Belgian holidaymakers and daytrippers, with a clean and commodious railway station on its main square, and through trains from as far away as Brussels, Liège and Maastricht.

If you wish to continue this tram ride — and what other stretch of coast is graced with 40 miles of continuous tracks — you will soon be transported to the quieter resorts of Wenduine and De Haan, with woodland and a golf course. To the right there will be glimpses of the sea; to the left, views across the grassy polders.

Bredene then heralds the start of the Ostend conurbation. The tram crosses harbour and canal bridges before coming to a rest next to the railway terminus on the edge of the old part of the town. Originally a small fishing port, Ostend became a resort with the opening of its casino in 1837 followed by the railway from Mecheln a year later. In the 1840s, the first steamers arrived from Dover, taking seven hours for the crossing. There is also a spa, horse-racing track and another broad sandy beach.

The Belgian coastal tramway runs from Knokke to De Panne

The tram continues along the intensively built-up coastal strip through Middelkerke and Westende before turning inland to cross the small River Ijzer at Nieuwpoort. This little town was destroyed in the 1914-1918 war but sensitively reconstructed afterwards, and you may feel like a stop here for refreshments, or to inspect the mighty sluices on the river.

Then, for the last leg of the journey, catch another westbound tram, returning quickly to the coast through the resorts of Nieuwpoort-Bad and Koksijde, the latter with its leafy avenues, abbey ruins, regional museum and the highest dune on the coast. De Panne, terminus of the tramway, is a small adjacent resort whose wide beach is the venue for sand-yachting.

If you do not want to return on the tram, you now have the option of a train back to Ghent from neighbouring Adinkerke; or an infrequent bus service across the border to the French village of Bray-Dunes and then on to the station at Dunkirk.

Furnes

by John Pickford

Furnes is ideal for travellers who want variety. Close by are the expansive beaches of the Belgian North Sea coast. Further down that same coastline, just across the French border, lie the evacuation beaches east of Dunkirk, a poignant reminder of war. Furnes itself, within its compact environs, offers a rich heritage of art, history and architecture. The Flemish form of its name is Veurne.

Tunnel travellers will probably include the town within a Flemish itinerary perhaps starting from Lille. From Lille-Flandre there is a two hourly service to Ghent (French:Gand) From Ghent an hourly service reaches Furnes in 70 minutes. From Brussels an hourly service reaches Ghent in 30 minutes. From Ypres (Flemish: Ieper) a change at Ghent is also involved. From Bruges an interesting and direct journey would involve a train to Ostend, the coastal tramway to La Panne and a subsequent train or bus to Furnes. The station is on the north side of the town and offers "Train + Cycle" facilities.

The resorts of the Belgian coast enjoy excellent beaches but variable weather, if not always warm and sunny then invariably bracing and invigorating. Furnes is a ten-minute journey from the coast by train.

An authentic way of reaching the beaches evacuated by British troops in May 1940 would be on foot. A cycle ride across the border would be equally energetic and evocative.

The Grand' Place is the historic heart of the town. Within easy walking distance can be found the Langhuis (1615) with its Gothic belfry, the 14th century Église St Walburge with its monumental choir, and the late 16th, early 17th century Hôtel de Ville, characteristically Renaissance Flemish and home to much Cordoban leatherwork bearing witness to the town's period of Spanish sovereignty. It was during the 17th century that the town enjoyed its greatest period of wealth. A modern day link with that past is the annual Procession of Penitents which dates back to 1637. Poets inspired by the town include Rilke while Jose van Gucht, Louis Barreta and Paul Delvaux have included Furnes in their artistic creations.

The predominant landscape within the vicinity of Furnes is one of canals and polders, water and pastures. Trees do not survive in this salty environment. Of interest in the locality are Furnes-Ambracht with its Bakery Museum, Dixmude and the polderland of De Moeren, three to four metres below sea level. There are many organised walking or cycle routes in the area. At the end of a strenuous day, local pâté de campagne, crêpes, gaufres and bière des Moines de Ste Sixte should fit the bill without inflating it.

Bruges

by John Pickford

Train travel to this bustling, though picturesque, city of 120,000 is easy. The station offers train and cycle facilities which are particularly appropriate in an environment blighted by the car. Bruges is 15 minutes from Ostend, 24 minutes from Ghent and an hour from Brussels. Trains in all directions are frequent. However, and whenever the traveller arrives in Bruges there is never the disappointment of a wasted journey. A brief bus ride or a 20 minute walk opens up the heart of the city which has had to live somewhat self-consciously with its claim to be the "Venice of the North".

Bruges can be seen by a tour-boat circling the waterways, from a horse drawn carriage, from a cycle or, preferably, on foot. It is invariably busy, perhaps too busy, with tourists of all nationalities. This is a tribute to the special charm of the city and to its accessibility.

There is water at every turning. In the Middle Ages, Bruges was an important port trading throughout the world. Its inner port was the Lac d'Amour, today the Minnewater, adjacent to the park and close by the Begijnhof. More than a day is needed to do justice to the squares, museums and palaces of historic Bruges. The Grand' Place is dominated by a belfry 83 metres high, housing a superb carillon. Within easy walking distance are the Provincial Palace, Hôtel de Ville (1376) 18th century Palais de Justice, the Basilique du Saint-Sang and Église Notre-Dame, one of the biggest churches in Belgium and the Netherlands. Saint Sauveur Cathedral has its Gothic roots in the 13th century. Among the host of museums, and of particular interest to the British visitor, is the Musée Brangwyn, commemorating the work of the artist Frank Brangwyn who died in 1956, aged 89.

The 14th century Hôtel de Ville, is one of many fine historic buildings in Bruges

From Bruges there are boat excursions to Ostend, Ghent and Damme. Damme is particularly well worth a visit. It was here in 1468 that Charles the Bold married Margaret of York and that the legendary Tyl Oilenspiegel — a l4th century jester and magician featured in a book of tales by Thomas Mürner in 1519 — lived. A short train journey reaches Lissewege and, beyond it, Zeebrugge. Other local tourist attractions include the abbeys at St André and St Tuidon, the Tillegembos, Parc Baudouin and Beisbroek Estate. Bruges has a persistent charm which the attentions of the frantic tourist hordes cannot sully. This is a city that deserves to be absorbed slowly.

Ghent

by Bill Collins

Old and new sit happily side by side in Ghent, capital of East Flanders. Prosperous inhabitants throng medieval streets and tourists are well catered for.

There are two main stations, Gent Sint Pieters and Gent Dampoort. Neither is very central, but the 20-minute walk to the city centre is pleasant enough, so you may choose not to catch the bus.

Make first for the 16th century Stadhuis (Town Hall) on the street called Botermarkt, right in the city centre. Admire the ornate façade and the Gothic spiral staircase but do not forget to collect a street map from the

Tourist Information Office housed there. Opposite the Town Hall is the 13th century Jorishof, one of the oldest hotels in Europe.

Just around the corner is St Baaf's Cathedral, where pride of place undoubtedly goes to Jan van Eyck's famous altarpiece, the *Adoration of the Holy Lamb* regarded as the pinnacle of early Flemish art.

On the same square as the cathedral is the Lakenhalle (Cloth Hall), a Gothic building formerly used by the commission that regulated the cloth industry. In the Middle Ages, Ghent turned wool (mostly from England) into cloth and became very rich as a result. Nowadays the Cloth Hall puts on an audiovisual documentary about the life of Charles V, Holy Roman Emperor, who was born in the city.

Nearby is the Belfort (Bell Tower), a symbol of the freedom of the city's people, crowned with a gilded dragon made in the 14th century. The view from the 300ft summit (luckily there is a lift) is excellent.

Go past the Sint Niklaas Kerk (St Nicholas's Church) over the River Leie (which we know as the Lys, as in Fleur de Lys) and turn right into Korenlei. The view over the river is the most famous in all of Flanders: all the houses on the Graslei, on the opposite bank, have the famous Flemish stepped gable, but in other respects their styles are vastly different, as are their ages (the oldest dates from 1130). In the face of such ornamentation, who can doubt the claim that in the 16th century Ghent was the second most powerful city in northern Europe, after Paris? This area is also the departure point for half-hour tours of the city by motor launch and of longer boat trips to the artists' village of Deurle with its Gustaaf de Smeets Museum of Flemish Expressionist Art.

Walk northwards along the Korenlei and its extension (J Breydelstraat), turn right and cross the bridge. On the left is the castle called 's-Gravensteen (The Count's Castle), a gloomy fortress modelled on the Crusader castles of the Levant and open to the public. It was home to the Counts of Flanders before being converted to dungeons and a place of execution. Before the castle gates stand the beautiful gabled houses of Sint Veerle Plein (St Veerle Square), giving no hint of the hangings and beheadings that used to take place here.

Such grimness is untypical of Ghent. Its citizens have an eye for style, true to the memory of their medieval forebears.

Antwerp

by Bill Collins

Antwerp (Anvers) offers a combination that no other Belgian city can match. European City of Culture in 1993, it has managed to retain a wealth of historic buildings and possesses cultural and entertainment facilities for all tastes, but remains a lived-in, working place. Its half-a-million inhabitants are open to outside influence but proud of their own heritage.

The Tourist Information Office is immediately outside the classical Centraal Station. Virtually all points of interest lie in a westerly direction, between here and the River Scheldt. Proceed down De Keyserslei and its extensions, Leystraat and Meir, and turn left into the pedestrianised Wapper. On the left is Rubens' House (1611), now one of Antwerp's 20 museums. The gardens and magnificent interior should not be missed. Beyond the far end of Wapper, a vast open-air market is held every Sunday morning, purveying all the basics but specialising in cage birds.

Next we head for the cathedral, crossing on the way the Groenplaats, a 19th century square containing a statue of Rubens. Beware the barely-audible trams which terminate here! The souvenir shops in the street leading from the main far left corner of the square, with their lace and chocolates, betray the proximity of the Gothic cathedral to the right, built between 1352 and 1521. It takes 600 steps to reach the top of the North Spire, containing the 6,434 kg Carolus Bell. Downstairs in the cathedral hang Rubens' triptych *Erection of the Cross*, *Christ's Resurrection* and *Deposition from the Cross*.

A short way on is the much photographed square, Grote Markt. You would not expect that the flamboyant 16th century façades and Flemish stepped gables were built at a time of decline. The dominant building is the Town Hall, whose interior (open to the public) is also of interest. Tourism has not been allowed to spoil this area.

Between the Grote Markt and the river is an intimate network of narrow streets with colourful names which translate into such as Eel Bridge and Cabbage Quay. A few 20th century houses scrupulously observe the style of the more numerous 16th century structures. Here and elsewhere in Antwerp, cobbles dictate the wearing of flat shoes.

A stone's throw away is the wide Scheldt. This particular stretch saw the landing of East Anglian wool in the 14th century, Spanish wine and luxury goods later. Now it is a jetty for the "Flandria" pleasure boats which will take you on a river trip.

Even the smallest Antwerp café offers a good choice of fare to revive you after all this pavement-pounding. As befits a large port, many of the local people are able to translate the menu for you. Take advantage of the café loos, because there are few of the public variety.

The best way back to central station is by "Metro" (actually trams running in tunnels) from Groenplaats to Diamanten (adjacent to Centraal Station). If you have time to spare, explore the streets south of Diamanten, which are not only the centre of the European diamond trade, but also home to Antwerp's Jewish community, whose shops can provide you with a delicious speciality for your journey, even on a Sunday.

Ypres

by John Pickford

Ypres is well served by hourly trains from Ghent, the journey taking just over the hour. Travellers from Brussels have an excellent service to Ghent. From Lille Flandre the journey to Ypres involves a change at Courtrai, each part of the journey taking about 30 minutes. For the British traveller Ypres is a town of poignant, sad memories of the Great War in which 250,000 British soldiers died on the battlefields of Flanders. Ypres itself was almost totally destroyed in the war. The town dates back to the tenth century and by the 13th century along with Ghent and Bruges, was one of the most important in Flanders. Today, its medieval glories and sophistication combine with a sober experience of the 20th century to create a blend of traditions so often found throughout Flanders.

In 1927 the Menin Gate was inaugurated on the spot where thousands of British troops left Ypres for the battlefields. On the cold stone of the gate are inscribed the names of 55,000 dead soldiers. Each evening at eight o'clock, the traffic stops as the last post is played, even now, in memory of those soldiers. The gate is an imposing, quiet and civilised tribute to the fallen. From it leads a walk along the ramparts, constructed by Vauban in another turbulent period. Open from April to November is the Musée du Souvenir 14-18 at the Halles aux Draps on the Grand' Place.

There is an ever present reminder of the Great War in the fields of Flanders, where 170 military cemeteries provide a resting place for those who died here. Not far from Ypres is Passchendaele which can be reached by bus (No 64A) from Ypres Station. Here is another museum.

Within Ypres itself The Halles aux Draps (Cloth Market) has been restored to its 1304 splendour and topped by a superb belfry — those who brave its 264 steps have an excellent view of the town. The Cathedral of St Martin has been rebuilt in its original 15th century style. British visitors may wish to visit the Memorial Church of St George built in 1929.

From Ypres stretch tourist routes best followed by cycle — the Hop route is a reminder that Belgium prides itself in its beer; the Hill route serves as a reminder that in this part of Flanders not all of the country is low, and the 14-18 route provides a solemn lesson in the futility of war. Flanders is a place in which to eat and drink well and local specialities include Anguille Vert (eels), Poule au pot (chicken casserole), and hochepot washed down with as fine a selection of strong beers as can be found anywhere.

The superbly preserved medieval Grande Place, Brussels

Brussels

by Tony Morris

Brussels is an international rail crossway and as such is a superb base from which to explore rather than a goal in itself. Its rail connections with the old cities of Belgium and neighbouring Netherlands, Germany, Luxembourg and France are, in the main, excellent. Yet its scope as a base for a varied holiday and for sorties to both historical towns and attractive countryside could be more widely appreciated.

The Belgian capital is reached in just under three hours from London via the Channel Tunnel. From Ostend it is just over an hour by hourly train or at the same frequency from the coast at Knokke. Both trains from the coast pass through Bruges (Brugge) and Ghent, thus giving a service every 30 minutes between Brussels and these marvellous cities.

The Ostend trains continue one hour eastwards to Liège and half of these go on to Cologne (Köln). Looking northwards there are too many fast and slow trains to count to Antwerp (a little over 30 minutes by the fast ones) and there is an hourly service to the great cities of western Holland, with Amsterdam only three hours away. Many of the Amsterdam trains start their journey in Paris, with a total of 12 a day between Brussels and the French capital.

South-eastwards from Brussels there are hourly trains to Namur and points in the Ardennes hills and Luxembourg, while six go on to Strasbourg in France and Basle in Switzerland. Lastly, a dense network of frequent services connects Brussels with other Belgian towns and cities.

The city is, then, a great place for railway touring. Most trains serve the three main stations on the north-south axis, Nord, Central and Midi, although a few of the international trains miss stopping at the Central Station. Those on the south east line call at the Quartier Léopold (QL) station in eastern Brussels and most of them also at Schuman station in the area housing the offices of the European Union (EU).

What, then, of Brussels itself? First, it is the capital of a three-language state with Flemish, French and German (there being German speaking cantons in the east). English is nearly a de facto national language, widely used as it is in business, industry and the EU. French is the language of most Brussels residents but Flemish (Brussels is an island surrounded by Flemish-speaking territory) is widely used in offices and shops. Add to this the tens of thousands of non-Belgians living here — EU and Nato staff and their families, the huge foreign press corps, foreign businessmen etc. — and Brussels is perhaps the most cosmopolitan city in the world.

Brussels is not the most beautiful of cities. It is frankly less attractive than some of its neighbours, notably Bruges, Antwerp, Malines

(Mechelen), Louvain (Leuven) and many easily accessible smaller ones. However, it does have much going for it, whether museums, art galleries (enough to keep aficionados happy for days on end), the superbly preserved medieval Grande-Place, best viewed when floodlit and clear of traffic (as it increasingly is).

It is a pleasure to relax in this ancient square and listen to a free open-air concert on the carillon of the Hôtel de Ville which dominates it. While exploring the narrow streets nearby, visitors invariably pay a call on Mannekin Pis, the cheeky, water-squirting little statue on the corner of rue du Chêne and rue de l'Etuve. Originally carved in 1619, the present statue is a 19th century replacement and is clothed in a variety of uniforms on special occasions.

Some may want to view the Berlaymont monster, the European Commission headquarters which is presently closed and nothing more than a shell. Another monster is the Atomium in the district of Heysel, a curious 350ft construction of tubes and balls intended to represent an atom and erected in 1958 for the World Exhibition. Its main merit is a classy self-service restaurant in its topmost "ball".

Talking of restaurants, the Delta guide lists 1,800 at all price levels, some marvellous value compared with the UK: nearly 80 in the price bracket BFr 500-800 (£10-£16) including half a bottle of wine. The hotels: they are not as cheap as a few years ago, but better value for money than in London.

Open spaces in the busy city centre are relatively few, the most notable being the small symmetrically designed Parc de Bruxelles between the Royal Palace and the Parliament, and the Botanical Garden at the north end of the heart-shaped boulevard around the central area. However, a tram ride (line 44) out to Tervuren to the east will take you through the edge of the great Forêt de Soignes.

In addition to its trams, Brussels boasts a metro system based on an east-west line serving Central and Schumann stations and branching out into the suburbs, with three north-south "pre-metro" lines formed by putting the trams into tunnels in the central area.

Currently a "direct" ticket, valid for one hour, costs Bfr50 but a "carnet" of ten costs Bfr290 and is usable not only on the metro and pre-metro but also on the SNCB in the Brussels area.

Whether or not Brussels really becomes some sort of "capital of Europe", it is coming up in the world as a cosmopolitan city and is no longer a "provincial" backwater. With its art, museums, concerts, opera, restaurants and friendly natives it is a city not to be readily passed by.

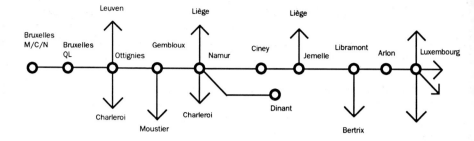

CHAPTER 7

Brussels-Luxembourg-Strasbourg

The "Euro-capitals" route

by Trevor Garrod

These three cities in three countries share the distinction of housing key institutions of the European Union, and you can travel by direct train between them.

Every hour, a red Belgian Inter City electric multiple unit train leaves from Brussels South (Midi or Zuid) for Luxembourg; and in the early morning, at midday and in the evening, an even faster train speeds from Brussels via Luxembourg to Strasbourg and from there on to Basle.

Our train is soon plunging into the tunnel built under Brussels in 1950, calling at the dimly-illuminated subterranean Central Station before re-emerging into daylight at Brussels North (Nord, Noord), a relatively modern station which also houses the national railway museum. We cross busy streets, curve past tightly packed housing and enter cuttings and more tunnels to reach the brightly lit platforms of Brussels Schumann — a station opened in the early 1970s to serve the adjacent European Union headquarters in the Palais du Berleymont.

The train gathers speed as it heads south-eastwards through the city's smarter suburbs, and is soon out in hilly wooded country, passing through the beechwoods of Soignes. A few miles away to the west, the Battle of Waterloo was fought in 1815. Calls at Ottignies and Gembloux show that we are now well within the French-speaking half of Belgium (Wallonia), and before long our train is descending into the Meuse valley, to reach, some 40 miles from Brussels, one of the chief cities of Wallonia, Namur.

At Namur's large and busy station, you can change for Liège, Mons and Charleroi, pausing perhaps to admire a small preserved steam engine in a siding. Namur (population 35,000) is worth a short stay, with its narrow shopping streets, baroque churches, 14th century belfry and domed cathedral. You can take a cablecar up to the imposing citadel on a wooded ridge dominating the valleys of the Meuse and its tributary, the Sambre. As the train curves out of Namur and rumbles over the river bridge, the view of the small city and its fortress is impressive.

Meuse Gorge

Then the tracks fork. Trains taking the right-hand fork are soon passing through the suburb of Jambes and then following the east bank of the Meuse along a wooded gorge. In summer in particular, through trains from Brussels use this line and call at stations serving resort villages like Profondéville, Godinne and Yvoir. The Meuse is also a working river, and you may see barges heading down towards the waterways of France right to the Mediterranean.

The train then crosses the river and comes to a halt in the modern station of Dinant, serving this attractive little town of some 7,000 people nestling below great cliffs on the opposite bank. There is much to do and see here — the Gothic church with its onion spire; the citadel high up on the cliff; caves to be explored and water sports to be tried. Then you could take a diesel railcar up the wooded Lesse valley to Houyet, Anseremme and beyond. The main line across the French border to Givet is now freight-only, but tourist trains operate on it from April to September. These services by steam or vintage diesel train are run by the Chemin de Fer à Vapeur des 3 Vallées and details are obtainable locally or from Jean-Marie Warzee, Chef du Mouvement CFV3V, rue de Namur 29, 5000 Beez-sur-Meuse. The company also operates steam trains between Mariembourg (served by a Société National de Chemin de Fer Belge branch from Charleroi) to Momignies and Treignes.

Into the Ardennes

Returning to our Inter City train at Namur, we take the left fork at Jambes and are soon climbing into hill country. This is the Famenne, which merges into the Ardennes, an upland area of woods and pastures with stone-built and slate-clad cottages and farms. There will be no more large towns for 100 miles.

Inter City trains call at the modern stone-built station of Ciney, some 18 miles from Namur, and then at Jemelle, junction for another scenic line northwards to Liège. The sidings at these and some other stations on the route contain waggons of local timber, while quarries also provide freight for the railway.

Now we are in the heart of the Ardennes, as our train continues to climb narrow valleys covered in trees, past tiny villages with, on higher ground, long vistas of distant forest ridges. As the train snakes its way up these lonely wooded valleys, past trickling brooks, the busy city of Brussels seems a world away. The little station of Poix-St Hubert, not served by Inter City trains, is railhead for the small town of St Hubert, famous for the basilica of its former abbey and a place of pilgrimage. In 683, the huntsman Hubert saw a vision on Good Friday and gave up his sport for the priesthood. He is now the patron saint of hunters and butchers.

We call at Libramont, a small town on a clear plateau, where it is possible to change to a branch-line diesel railcar southwards to Bertrix or north-eastwards to Bastogne, a town popular with American visitors with memories of their army's stand there in the Battle of the Bulge in 1944.

Then the countryside becomes more gently undulating as we swing eastwards, pass a marshalling yard and slow down to approach Arlon, a town of 14,000 on a small hill, dominated by the churches of St Martin and St Donat. On a clear day it is possible to enjoy a view of four countries from the latter's tower. Arlon was the Roman Orolaunum, and you can see Roman remains in the museum of local history. This town, like other places on the line, is a good centre from which the more energetic can explore the surrounding countryside on foot or by bicycle — followed perhaps by generous quantities of beer and Ardennes ham.

Arlon station was built on a rather grand scale as a frontier post — but customs controls on this border have long since disappeared and the most you are likely to see is a change of crew before the train proceeds over curving tracks south-eastwards into the Grand Duchy of Luxembourg.

Some subtle changes come over the gently undulating plateau. The clean neat villages with their church spires have a certain Teutonic look. Although our train is speeding along, we may also catch sight of station names like Kleinbettingen and Capellen, which look distinctly German.

Presently we approach city suburbs, then sidings and the junctions with lines from France merging in from the right. Our train rounds a curve and draws into Luxembourg station.

The building, with its clock tower, is ornate and has a distinctive character; while its facilities include several shops, a reasonable buffet and even showers. To get to know this small capital city of an independent state no larger than an English county, take a few minutes' walk along the avenue de la Gare. Suddenly before you is a spectacular view of a deep gorge with houses, gardens and the tiny river Pétrusse on its floor. On the other side, reached by two fine bridges, the old city rises on a fortified ridge dominated by slender church and cathedral spires. Luxembourg has a certain fairy-tale, some might say, Ruritanian, air when approached from this direction.

After exploring the old city, with its casemates built by Austrian occupiers, castle ruins and Renaissance Palace of the Grand Duke, go to see the other Luxembourg. You can take a city bus — notices on bus shelters exhort you to do so and help protect the environment. North of the old city approached by the stark red steel Pont Grand-Duchesse Charlotte, high above the Alzette gorge, the Plateau du Kirchberg displays a very different aspect of the capital, peppered as it is with modern glass, steel and concrete buildings of various European institutions established here, starting with the Coal and Steel Community in 1952. This little city, fought over and occupied by French, Spaniards, Austrians and Prussians during its long history, is now a symbol of European unity.

Trains continuing to Strasbourg reverse out of Luxembourg and head south across the border via industrial Thionville to Metz, described in Chapter 4. They then head east across the more lightly populated plateau of Lorraine to join the east main line at Reding. A short tunnel through the heights of the Vosges brings the line into the spectacular wooded valley of the little River Zorn, from which it emerges at Saverne, a pleasant town overlooked by vineyards and a ruined castle, on to the floor of the Rhine valley and a brisk final run to Strasbourg.

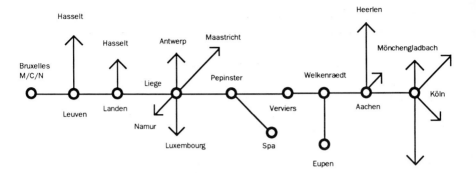

CHAPTER 8

Brussels-Cologne

by Trevor Garrod

This 140-mile line, with its fastest trains taking a little over two and a half hours for the journey, dates from the early 1840s and was one of the core routes of Europe long before the Channel Tunnel was built. It is now even more important and plans have been drawn up to build stretches of new high-speed track along this corridor.

At the moment, two Inter City trains every hour head north out of Brussels, veer to the east, past marshalling yards, and then out to the suburb of Zaventem, where a line branches off northwards to serve the international airport. A short run through open country follows before the train slows on the curve approaching Leuven (pronounced Ler-ven; French "Louvain") an ancient town of some 31,000 people, best known for its university dating from 1425 and the seat of the scholar Erasmus. There is a wealth of old houses and churches from the 13th and 14th centuries, many reconstructed after war damage, and a splendid 15th century Gothic town hall. A walk from the station straight along Bondgenotenlaan brings us right into the historic heart.

The railway now takes a south-westerly course through the gently rolling farmland of Brabant and the next town, Tienen, has less of historic interest but, instead, boasts one of the largest beet processing factories in the world, producing over 200,000 tonnes of sugar every year.

Seven miles further is the junction of Landen, where semi-fast trains call and divide, with part of the train veering northwards on the branch to Hasselt and then over a section reopened to passengers in the early 1980s to serve the car-making town of Genk.

As our main line train speeds across the flatland towards Waremme, the next small town, we cross the language divide and are back in Wallonia, French-speaking Belgium. Before long we reach the suburbs of Liège, the largest city of Wallonia and third largest in Belgium. It is a useful centre from which to explore a fascinating area and is described in more detail in chapter 13. Some trains head north from Liège to Maastricht. If we are on a train to Germany or Eupen, however, we are soon rumbling across the River Meuse and curving our way up the valley of the Vesdre towards the textile centre of Verviers, dominated by a motorway viaduct at its western end. The hilly scenery is pleasant, but the towns and villages are not among the most architecturally attractive in the country.

The line curves its way northwards to Aix-la-Chapelle — or Aachen — the German border city which can also be used as a centre for exploring this region where three countries meet. From Aachen, it is a further 45 miles eastwards through the foothills of the Eifel, to Cologne. Electrification of this route was completed in 1966.

You may, however, prefer to change at Aachen for the InterRegio service, introduced in 1991, which makes its way across to the industrial cities of the Ruhr and the rich agricultural plain of Westphalia, before turning southwards to Kassel and Fulda in the very heart of Germany. The InterRegios are the German equivalent of our Express Sprinter trains; but, unlike our Sprinters, they are full-length loco-hauled trains with bistro bars and more generous facilities for bicycles. They complement the fast Inter City trains with which they connect at many points en route.

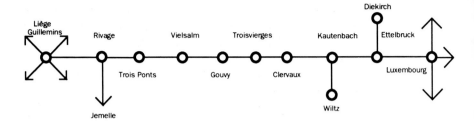

CHAPTER 9

Luxembourg-Liège

by Michael Oakley and Trevor Garrod

Unlike its neighbour, Alsace-Lorraine, Luxembourg has had a surprisingly stable history in a sometimes turbulent region. Its geographical position has always made it a natural meeting of ways, being at one side of the bowl formed by the Moselle and Saar rivers, between the Ardennes and more distant Vosges ranges of hills. Although frequently changing hands, it seems to have been recognised by successive owners as an asset not for stripping. Thus it grew to civic status from 1224, Duchy status from 1354, and finally Grand Duchy status from 1815. It remains above all else an administrative centre, becoming the headquarters of the European Steel Cartel in 1926, though perhaps best known to many for its idiosyncratic radio station.

Early plans for a British-financed "Great Luxembourg Railway" in the 1830s, as part of a direct route from Antwerp to the Near East, came to nought; and it was not until relatively late that the Grand Duchy joined the burgeoning European network. The first railway to be built on its territory was from Arlon via Luxembourg to Thionville, opened in 1859. This was the first route to be electrified, in 1956, and it remains an important trunk line. The main express services over it are inevitably operated by the Belgian and French railways, leaving the CFL to compensate by working a range of intensive local trains. The exception, the one line that could be considered at least half Luxembourg's own, is its route north towards the Belgian frontier near Gouvy, opened in stages between 1862 and 1867.

This double-track line is characterised by its clean, neat stations serving a succession of small towns and villages. The main historical town en route is Clervaux, a place of barely 2,000 people, whose picturesque houses and hotels are sandwiched in a narrow valley, dominated by a castle dating from the 12th century. Also of interest is an abbey on the plateau to the west of the town. Well-appointed tourist facilities include a camp site and indoor

89

swimming pool by the river.

A short branch serves Diekirch, whose church traces its origins back to the seventh century, while the museum testifies to earlier Roman occupation. Of the more modern buildings there is the brewery whose product is consumed throughout the Grand Duchy.

Further north, at the junction of Kautenbach amid wooded hillsides, a picturesque single-track branch follows the tree-lined valley of the Wiltz to the small town of that name, whose 17th century castle and mediaeval quarter huddle on a spur of land 500 ft above the newer town on the valley floor.

Let us return to the main line. Through trains take some two and a half hours to cover the 160kms between Luxembourg and Liège, while others cover just part of the route. For most of its length, the line follows river valleys, first the Alzette, then its scenic tributary the Sûre, and finally the little Clerve. Construction was hindered by the need for frequent tunnels to keep the curvature under reasonable control. Although lacking the feeling of rolling expanse that characterises the Arlon route through the Belgian Ardennes, this one is much more attractive in a localised self-contained sort of way, as it climbs over a narrow ridge at the centre of the Ardennes woods. The same landscape then persists as the line winds down the valley of the Salm, following its waters into the valley of the Amblève at Trois-Ponts and then joining the

The 13.08 express from Liège to Luxembourg near Lintgen

secondary route from Jemelle, to follow the Ourthe to the main line junction at Angleur.

Operationally the line was until 1993 a mixture, with electric local services as far as Ettelbrück and mostly diesel working beyond. Electrification of the main cross-border service has now begun though this may well require some interesting motive power development for interworking with the differing SNCF and SNCB systems.

At the Belgian end of the route, arrival in the bustling city of Liège gives very much the feeling of entering a faster world. At the time of writing the only long-distance train on the route is the solitary through coach operation between Basle and Maastricht in each direction, but on the pattern of European services generally in recent years, the completion of the electrification could well see this route carrying more such passenger trains.

CHAPTER 10

Land of three countries

Ardennes, Eifel and Dutch Alps

by Simon Norton and Trevor Garrod

On the main line from the Channel Tunnel to Central Europe lies the city of Liège, gateway to one of the continent's most fascinating regions. As well as visiting historic cities such as Maastricht, Aachen, Luxembourg and Trier, you can move away to explore some of the byways and scenery. A good map — easily obtainable locally — is strongly advised, to maximise your enjoyment.

Liège itself may be used as a touring centre, since six rail routes converge there and it has all the facilities you would expect in a city of half a million people. There are historic churches and museums, the former Palace of the Prince-Bishops and the cathedral to admire. Then you can watch the shipping on the mighty River Meuse that winds its way through the city; or climb steep, narrow streets to the citadel and admire the view below. Liège is also the birthplace of the creator of the detective, Inspector Maigret, Georges Simenon, whose early career as a local journalist gave him ideas for many of his novels.

The scenery starts soon after leaving Liège, whether one continues on the main line to Aachen and Cologne, or turns south towards Luxembourg (described in the previous chapter). Between these two lines lies the highest part of the Ardennes. There are two passenger branch lines: one leaves the main line at Pepinster (you can also change at Verviers Central) for the town of Spa, which gave its name to the English generic term for resorts based on mineral water springs.

The single-track branch threads its way along a wooded valley to reach Spa station with its roof which dates from an era when the rich and powerful descended upon this small town to take the waters. It was also used by Kaiser Wilhelm II as his headquarters during the First World War, and it was from this station in November 1918 that his royal train took him, via Liège, to Eijsden, just across the border, and exile in the Netherlands.

In these more peaceful times, Spa attracts many visitors to its shops, hotels and cafés, the town nestling in a beautiful position surrounded by wooded hills among which pleasant walks can be made. Beyond the hills to the south is the motor-racing circuit of the Francorchamps — so Spa is a little less peaceful on race days.

The other branch from the Liège-Aachen line leaves at the small border town of Welkenraedt, crosses the motorway and leads to Eupen — though the track continues well beyond that. This very scenic line is the Vennbahn, whose name derives from the German term for the area (French: Fagnes). The local authority is developing the line as a tourist attraction. Details of special trains to Monschau and Büllingen can be obtained from Eupen or Aachen tourist offices. They are very popular and advance booking is strongly recommended.

Eupen, a town of 15,000 people, is the largest centre in German-speaking Belgium. Indeed, the area was part of Germany from the end of the Napoleonic Wars until 1919, when it was given to Belgium under the Treaty of Versailles.

Eupen station was closed in the 1950s but reopened, rebuilt and the line electrified in 1984. It is now the terminus for local trains from Spa and some Inter City trains from Ostend. A short walk brings you to the centre of this pleasant town, whose hilly streets link two narrow valleys and which is dominated by a church with bulbous, German-looking spires. To the south are the densely wooded slopes of the Hertogenwald, through which a road climbs to the Signal de Bottrange, the highest point in Belgium.

To explore this part of Belgium further, go by bus. To save money on the buses in Belgium or the Netherlands, buy tickets in advance at a railway station: ask for a "Z-Carte" (in Belgium) or "Strippenkaart" (in the Netherlands). As you board, show this to the driver, who will cancel part of it according to your destination.

Here are some of the more interesting bus routes serving the area, including the cathedral town of Malmédy (Railheads are starred)

45a Trois Ponts* -Malmédy-Büllingen-Manderfeld

390 Verviers* -Baraque Michel-Büllingen

395 Verviers* -Malmédy-St Vith-Reuland

396 Malmédy -Eupen* -Kelmis-Vaals

Vaals is actually in the Netherlands. (Note: it is not in Holland, any more than Glasgow is in England.) However, it adjoins the German border, and buses to Aachen are available at the other side.

From Liège you also have the choice of train or bus to Maastricht — a city whose name is known to everyone in the European Union since the conference there in December 1991. In summer you can also reach it by boat along the Meuse, which changes to the Maas as it crosses the frontier. After exploring the narrow streets of the old city, many of them pedestrianised, and its medieval churches, ramparts and other old buildings, you may like to relax at one of the cafés of the imposing Market Place where, on Saturdays and public holidays, carillon concerts are given at the City Hall. Maastricht is also much visited for its hundreds of specialist shops and Wednesday and Friday markets.

A short train ride to the east of Maastricht is Valkenburg, that most un-Dutch of towns in the valley of the small Geul river. It has developed as a very popular inland resort for Dutch people who will find hills a novelty. There are amusements for all the family in this picturesque town of 12,000, dominated by its 13th century castle ruins. The station is also built in castellated style and, dating from 1850, is said to be the oldest surviving station building in the Netherlands.

The train continues to Heerlen — a larger town but of less character, having grown mostly over the last century on what was until the 1960s the small Dutch coalfield. The direct line from Valkenburg to Aachen has been closed and trains to Germany rerouted via Heerlen and a reopened border at Kerkrade.

For those who imagine the Netherlands to be just dykes and windmills, a visit to South Limburg, this most southerly part of the country, is quite an eye-opener. These gentle hills — the "Dutch Alps"— reach a height of some 400 feet in the excellent walking country where Belgium, Germany and the Netherlands meet.

Aachen is also a historic city, centred on its massive cathedral, and was the capital of the Emperor Charlemagne in the ninth century.

Düren, just beyond Aachen, is the junction for the Rurtalbahn, a branch line that goes up the Rur valley (not to be confused with the more famous Ruhr) to Heimbach in the Eifel hills. Not far from Heimbach there is a system of lakes on which cruises are run in the summer. One of these, the Urftalsperre, is a military training area only accessible by boat. Various bus routes from Aachen, Düren, Heimbach, possibly with a change at Simmerath or picture-postcard Monschau (which we met earlier on the Vennbahn), provide access to the lakes; or it's a moderate walk from Heimbach.

North of Aachen is a steam railway which runs on summer Sundays. The nearest station is Geilenkirchen, on the electrified line to Mönchengladbach, and there is a connecting bus link to the line at Gillrath. Aachen is also served by regular buses to Eupen and Heerlen, but the most interesting route is the "Eifel-Ardennen-Express" which runs daily to Trier via Verviers, St Vith and Prüm, providing a cross-country facility on a corridor without rail services.

CHAPTER 11

Dutch railtrail

by Bill Collins

The Dutch Rail Trail can be pursued in smart, clean and frequent electric trains that link the principal towns and cities of the Netherlands.

Your entry into the country is most likely to be at Roosendaal, on one of the Inter City trains that run every hour throughout the day from Brussels to Amsterdam. After speeding through the extensively built-up area north of the Belgian capital, calling only at Mechelen and at Berchem on the outskirts of Antwerp, you will soon be in that typical Dutch landscape of flat pastureland, straight canals and grassy dykes; though clogs and windmills are less in evidence these days.

Roosendaal is the junction for the port of Vlissingen (Flushing, as we used to call it) and picturesque medieval Middelburg; or you can catch a cross-country service via Tilburg (for De Efteling theme park), Nijmegen, Arnhem and Zwolle in the eastern part of the country.

A dozen more miles across flat land brings you to Lage Zwaluwe, an important junction in the open countryside, where the main line from Maastricht and Eindhoven trails in and the train slows on approach to the Moerdijk Bridge. This is a long girder construction, with a road bridge just to the west of it, crossing the broad estuary of the Maas, known at this point as the Hollands Diep. As the train rumbles over the murky waters, look upstream to the wooded islands of the Biesbos, a bird reserve.

Back on land, the train soon reaches Dordrecht, and then its counter-part, Zwijndrecht, shipbuilding towns on the banks of the Oude Maas, another of the rivers of the vast delta of the Maas and the Rhine. Note the ornate church tower close to the Dordrecht riverside — tall towers, often with intricate masonry, are a feature of Dutch towns and villages, just as they are of those in Flanders.

The great conurbation of Rotterdam is soon upon us, and new tracks have been added alongside this busy line. Freight sidings appear, you pass the Feyenoord football stadium on the right, cross the Nieuwe Maas — yet another busy waterway of the Delta — before curving round the city centre on a viaduct to reach Rotterdam's modern Central Station. In 1993 this bottleneck was eased by the opening of a rail tunnel under the river.

Six trains an hour leave Rotterdam Central for The Hague, half of them also calling at Delft, arriving at The Hague HS (Hollandse Spoor) station. There is an alternative route from Rotterdam Hofplein, a two-platform ter-minus two streets away from the main station, to The Hague CS (Central).

If you have time, it is worthwhile to take a ride on the Zoetermeer Line, opened in the 1970s to serve the new town that was built around the old village of Zoetermeer, just inland from The Hague. The line makes two circles round the estates of modern flats, with a dozen small stations equipped with plenty of cycle racks.

The main line continues a few miles inland from the coast, and parallel to it, to the old university town of Leiden, with four trains every hour. Two of these then continue on the old route up to Haarlem before turning inland to Amsterdam, while the other two take the new route inland, constructed in the 1980s to serve Schiphol Airport. Your train shoots across the polder formed in the 19th century by the draining of the Haarlemer Meer, before entering a tunnel, pausing at the station below the airport terminal, and emerging into the suburbs of Amsterdam. Note the ultra-modern Sloterdijk station, just before Amsterdam Central.

You are now halfway around the circle of urban areas often referred to as the Randstad. To the north-east are the vast new areas of land reclaimed from the Ijsselmeer over the past 40 years. You can ride across this new land on the railway built to serve the new towns of Almere and Lelystad. It brings home the significance of the saying "God made heaven and earth, but the Dutch made Holland".

To continue the rail trail, catch one of the trains from Amsterdam to Utrecht, of which there are at least six an hour. For the first few miles, you will speed through modern suburbs, before reaching a more pastoral landscape where the railway follows the Amsterdam-Rhine Canal for many miles to reach Utrecht, headquarters of the Nederlandse Spoorwegen (Dutch Railways) and a key junction.

The final stage of the trail takes you back out of Utrecht, across more green fields intersected by canals. By now you will have come to expect trains in this country to run at frequent, predictable intervals, and this line is no exception. The main intermediate town is Gouda, famous for its cheese. Many trains also call at Rotterdam Alexander, a modern suburb where you can take a tram into the city centre.

Back in Rotterdam, you may like to complete your Dutch rail trail with a trip on the city's underground, opened in stages from 1968. It consists of two lines crossing at right angles in the city centre, the longest stretch going under the river and surfacing in the southern suburbs, with views from its embankment across the industrial and dockland areas.

Your lasting impression of the rail trail will probably be of interesting old cities, ultra-modern urban and suburban areas, a wealth of greenery and water, plenty of bicycles and modern internationally minded people using an attractive and efficient public transport system.

Rotterdam

Modern industry on the grand scale can draw the visitor as surely as any listed building. Rotterdam has proved the point by imaginative tourist provision at its port (at 9,776 hectares the largest in the world). And, while the city suffered wholesale destruction in the hostilities of 1940, no fewer than 12 museums now exist to show the way things were.

Among these, the Museum Boymans-van Beuning (Mathenesserlaan nos18-20, a tram ride from the Central Station) is surely a must, with paintings by Bruegel, Rembrandt, Rubens and others. A one-stop eastbound Metro journey from Eendrachtplein station (near the Museum) takes you to Churchillplein station, which is within 300 metres of the Maritiem Museum Prins Hendrik at Leuvehaven no 1, the adjacent Museum Ship called *Buffel* (Buffalo) and the Historisch Museum Schielandshuis (at Korte Hoog Straat no 31) which describes the daily art and life of Rotterdam.

If you walk further up Korte Hoog Straat and turn right into Hoog Straat, you will see not only a typical Dutch street market but also an attractive old canal, Delftse Vaart, and on the canal's east side, the square containing the St Lawrence Church (Sint Laurens Kerk or Grote Kerk), a 15th century cruciform basilica, sensitively restored between 1951 and 1968.

To see the grandeur of the port, make for Willemsplein (on the route of tram 5). One-and-a-half-hour-long boat tours of the Port of Rotterdam depart from here throughout the year, while in July and August whole day trips are made to Europoort, with its oil installations, and even further afield to the Deltawerken (Delta Works) the vast coastal defences erected after the islands of South Holland and Zeeland were flooded in 1953. The Dutch know no peers in this type of civil engineering.

For another angle on the city, you could ascend the Euromast at Parkhaven no 20 (about 700 metres from the quay where you disembarked). The Space Needle, an external rotating lift car, will take you up to the top section to the 220 metre Crow's Nest from where, on a clear day, you can see not only Rotterdam but Delft and The Hague also. A short walk, or ride in tram 6 or 9, will take you to Delfshaven, one of the oldest parts of Rotterdam, and the port of departure of the Pilgrim Fathers in 1620. The church where they worshipped still stands.

Rotterdam is also a good base for a trip to the world-famous windmills at Kindedijk, about seven miles distant. Catch a bus from the Central Station. The 19 mills, built in 1740 to drain the surrounding polder, operate on Saturday afternoons, when one of them is open to the public.

Delft

Situated between Rotterdam and The Hague, Delft is much smaller and more intimate than either. In its Golden Age with its houses and narrow tree-lined canals, it epitomises our idea of a graceful, old Dutch town. This tour can be made on foot.

From the station, cross the wide canal, turn right and immediately left. Cross the first canal you come to, but turn left along the far (east) side of the second, called Koornmarkt. Turn right into Oude Langendijk and immediately left, into the historic Market Place. At the near end is the Town Hall (Stadhuis) rebuilt in 1618 in Dutch Renaissance style, and worth entering (Monday to Friday) for its 16th to 18th century paintings.

At the other end of the market place is the New Church (Nieuwe Kerk), a monumental edifice with a tower 355 feet high. The ornate black and white marble tomb of William of Orange should not be missed.

Around the corner from the Nieuwe Kerk, in the street called Kerk Straat, is the Atelier de Candelaer, one of three workshops in the town that still produce the famous Delft ware. It is open to the public.

Go back to the Markt, leave it via the west (Town Hall) end, cross the first canal, turn left and immediately right. The street called Oude Delft ("Old Delft"), running either side of the second canal, contains much of interest. At number 167 there is a fine portal, surmounted by nine colourful coats of arms, while at number 215 is a convent whose church has fine baroque decorations.

To return to the station, go southwards along Oude Delft and turn right into Babara Steeg. Turn right and immediately left (almost straight across, in fact) and the station lies before you.

The Hague

Although the Dutch monarchs are inaugurated in the capital, Amsterdam, it is The Hague that contains the official residence of the House of Orange, the Houses of Parliament and the government ministries — buildings which have witnessed many of the decisive moments of the country's history. Many works of art from the Netherlands' Golden Age, acquired with the proceeds of officially sponsored imperial enterprise, are on display in the city.

The Hague is called Den Haag in Dutch — an abbreviation of its official name, 's-Gravenhage, which is never used in speech. It is a flat, compact city of about half a million people (including suburbs). Your train may stop at Den Haag HS, but it is advisable to continue to Den Haag CS (Central

Station) and pick up a city map at the tourist office on the station forecourt.

I would then hire a bicycle (also from the station precincts), but you may prefer to use the good bus or tram system. Make first for the Binnenhof (Inner Court) in the city centre. The late 13th century Ridderzaal (Knights' Hall) in the north-east corner of the Binnenhof is The Hague's oldest building and the largest secular Gothic structure in Western Europe. It was under its beamed ceiling that the Netherlands declared its independence from Spain, and it is here that Queen Beatrix officially opens Parliament on the third Tuesday of September. An exhibition at Binnenhof, number 8a, describes the development and operation of Parliament and the monarchy, and is good preparation for a guided tour of either House. Just beyond the elegant gate at the north end of the Binnenhof is the Mauritshuis, a repository for much of the work of Vermeer (including his *View of Delft*), Hals, Rembrandt and others.

Retrace your steps through the Binnenhof and head for the Grote Kerk (The Great, or St Jacob's Church) with its hexagonal tower, unique in the Netherlands. The nearby Gevangenpoort (Prisoners' Gate) now houses a museum dedicated to torture!

You are now very near the street called Noordeinde (North End), The Hague's most fashionable shopping street. At its western end, go straight on, cross the canal (one of several in the city) and into See Straat. On the right, at number 65b, is the Panorama Mesdag. At almost 300 feet in circumference, it is the biggest cyclorama (panoramic painting) in Europe. It depicts the fishing village of Scheveningen in 1880. Later we shall see how much this has changed!

Our next stop is at Madurodam, where the Netherlands' most famous buildings have been recreated outdoors, on a scale of one to 25. Children will like it, particularly the moving models such as Eindhoven railway station. The displays are lit at night. Madurodam is between the centre of The Hague and Scheveningen, our next and last objective.

No longer a fishing village, Scheveningen is the North Sea's largest resort, with facilities for all tastes and pockets. The sandy beach is cleaned every night, the shops open seven days per week and there is no hint of dowdiness.

Amsterdam

As capitals go, Amsterdam is a small city (population 700,000), yet only three European cities attract more visitors. Its character derives from its concentric canals, which separate markedly different districts. Wherever you go in Amsterdam, you will find a vibrant, tolerant place. There are pockets of seediness, but it is a safe city by international standards.

The following walking tour of Amsterdam's central area takes in only a

Barbara Allen

A typical scene in old Amsterdam with canal, bridge and barge

fraction of the city's sights, but conveys its essence. Leave the flamboyantly decorated Central Station by the main (south) exit and beware of trams as you cross the station square. Go down Damrak, the street ahead of you which contains the Beurs van Berlage (Berlage's Exchange) designed by the father of modern Dutch architecture, H P Berlage, in the late 19th century. Its style is in stark contrast to that of Central Station, roughly its contemporary. A little further on is Dam Square, the very centre of the city. The national monument in the middle of the square is a memorial to the victims of the Second World War.

Across the square is the Koninglijk Paleis (Royal Palace), notable mainly for its Burgerzaal (Citizens' Hall) filled with marble carvings, chandeliers and Art Deco, while inside luxury vies with kitsch. At the far end of the street is the Rembrandtplein, lined with pavement cafés dispensing the proverbial Amsterdam conviviality. There is no traffic here: the noise comes from buskers. At night it becomes a cacophony.

Leave the square at the opposite end, go up the Amstelstraat, over the bridge, past the controversial new Town Hall on the left, and you come to the famous flea market on Waterlooplein, once the heart of the Jewish district. Here you can find anything from bicycle parts to Indonesian clothing. From Waterlooplein Metro station there is a direct line to Amsterdam Central, which is where we came in.

Amsterdam's Metro was opened between 1977 and 1982, and comprises just 18km of route. In addition, however, the city has 123.8km of surface tramway comprising 16 different routes.

Though perhaps exhausting, this initial tour is not exhaustive. In Amsterdam it could never be. Nor is it all "high" culture. The main omissions of course are the Rijksmuseum, with its Halses and Rembrandts, and the nearby van Gogh museum dedicated to works by the popular artist. Not only are they outside the central area, they deserve at least a day to themselves. Catch a number 170 bus from the Central Station.

Utrecht

Utrecht, capital of the province of the same name, is at the centre of the Netherlands' road, rail and waterway network. It is also a very old city, which has played a prominent rôle in the country's history.

The indoor shopping centre surrounding the Central Station claims to be Europe's largest, but character and beauty are elsewhere in the city. This is another Dutch city that needs more than a day, so my one-day walking-tour omits a lot.

Leave the station by the east (main) exit, pass the indoor shopping malls and you emerge outdoors in an extensive pedestrianised area. Cross the square and proceed up Drie Haringstraat. Turn left into Oude Gracht. This runs alongside one of Utrecht's picturesque canals, unusual in the Netherlands in that the roadway runs high above water level, with the canal bank providing access to cellars under the street. Much of the canal bank is occupied by restaurant tables, from where you can watch the pleasure craft. Cross the canal by the first bridge, turn left up the other bank and you will soon come to Huis Drakenburg, a late 13th century house with a rebuilt façade.

Go back along the east side of the canal until you have passed five bridges, then turn left into the Dom Plein (Cathedral Square). The Cathedral Tower is Utrecht's most famous landmark and at 112 metres the tallest church tower in the Netherlands. It is quite a climb to the top, but the view is splendid. A hurricane blew down the cathedral nave in 1674, isolating the tower, but the surviving chapels and cloisters deserve a visit.

Walk along Achter de Dom ("Behind the Cathedral") and you will come to the Paushuize (Pope's House). This elegant 16th century house was built for Adrian VI, the only Dutch Pope, although he never lived in it.

Proceeding via Pausdam, Kromme Nieuwe Gracht, Jeruzalemstraat and turning into Herenstraat, you come to the Stadsbuitengracht (External Canal). Lining the canal's near side, where the city's defence once stood, are some fine gardens, set in a quiet area. Turn right, keeping to the canal bank, and you soon reach, on the left, the bridge (Malie Brug) leading to the Dutch Railway Museum, which cannot rival York's railway museum, but nevertheless contains plenty of rolling stock.

Less specialised tastes may prefer the Centraal Museum which is approached by first continuing along the canal bank until it is joined on your right by a smaller canal called Nieuwe Gracht, and then walking along the street (not the canal bank) leading away from the latter. The Museum, at Agnietenstraat no1, contains paintings by Utrecht masters, a doll's house from 1680 and many displays of Utrecht's history. On leaving, turn left into Agnietenstraat, then first right, and the picturesque canal bank will lead you back to the city centre.

PART THREE

GERMANY

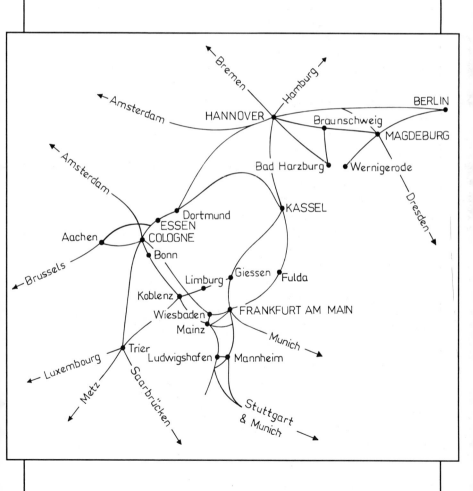

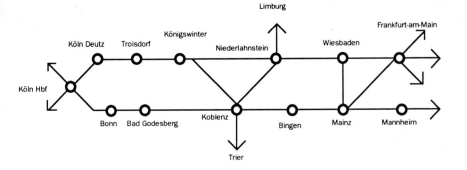

CHAPTER 12

The Rhine and Mosel valleys

Cologne to Mainz

by Paul Burton

Where we have Old Father Thames, the Germans have "Vater Rhein" — the great river which rises in the Alps, forms the border between Germany and Switzerland and then sweeps its majestic way northwards. For centuries it has been both a natural frontier and a major routeway of Europe.

Between Mainz and Cologne the river has to pass through uplands and has created for itself a gorge with picturesque towns and villages on its banks, vineyards up its sides and castles on its heights.

You may travel through this gorge by Köln-Düsseldorfer steamer or by train, as there is an electrified main line on either bank.

Three Inter City trains run along the Rhine Valley every hour. All of them take the left bank route, electrified in 1959, stopping only at Bonn and Koblenz. They are interspersed with stopping trains, should you wish to linger in this scenic area, and even combine your train ride with a boat trip. Remember the German trains "drive on the right", so sit on the left of the train for the best views! Regular services also use the right bank route and ferries cross the river, providing yet more ways of seeing places of interest.

View from Rheinfels Castle with road, rail and river traffic below

The journey from Cologne to Bonn by local train is described on page 110. The main line runs slightly away from the river to Bonn, after describing a great curve round to the west of the city, affording views of its cathedral towers from a variety of angles. South of Bonn, the line follows the river fairly closely for 130km, in one of the classic rail journeys of Europe.

Twenty kilometres south of Bonn is Remagen, the site of a strategic bridge, constructed during the First World War, which collapsed during the Second World War. It was not destroyed by the Germans, unlike all the others along the Rhine, and American troops were able to use it to establish a base on the right bank. Its collapse occurred after only ten days, due to overloading.

High above the town of Remagen is the Apollinariskirche, a miniature version of Cologne Cathedral, with frescoes of the lives of St Apollinaris, Jesus and the Virgin Mary.

The River Ahr joins the Rhine at Remagen, and a railway runs up its valley as far as Kreuzberg. The Ahrtal (Ahr Valley) is one of the most beautiful parts of Germany. The towns to see by train are Ahrweiler and Altenahr, and there are numerous signposted walks throughout the valley.

Andernach is reached shortly before the city of Koblenz. In 1988,

Andernach celebrated its 2,000th birthday, making it, not surprisingly, one of the oldest towns in Germany. The main attraction is its system of fortifications. These 13th century walls have weathered the passage of time remarkably successfully, and you can walk around them. The castle was blown up in 1688, but much of it has survived. Look out for the 15th century Round Tower.

Koblenz, with a population of 107,000, is the largest centre of the Rhine Gorge, lying at the point where the Mosel flows in from the south-west. All trains stop here, and railway bridges across the Rhine also enable right bank trains to call. Koblenz is also an ancient city — the Romans called it Confluens — and one that is popular as a touring centre. Indeed, the first Baedeker guide was published here in 1823. Its position gives the city a warm, indeed sultry, climate; and in the days when the Germans had African colonies (up to 1919), it was common for their troops to be trained here before being shipped to the tropics.

Most tourists in Koblenz will visit the Deutsches Eck (German Corner), a large open space where the two rivers join. From here can be seen a steady flow of freight barges along the Rhine. Sightseeing boats travel along both rivers. The other major sight of the city is the church of St Kastor, 800 years old.

On the opposite bank of the Rhine, at the top of a great cliff, is the fortress of Ehrenbreitstein. At the foot is a small station on the right bank line; and a chair lift takes visitors to the summit.

Koblenz and the Lahn Valley are described in Chapter 15

From Koblenz the hills draw in with a vengeance and the spectacular gorge begins. This is the Rhine of popular imagination and, despite geographical difficulties, the Inter City express speeds south. Keep your eyes open to take everything in!

The castle at Braubach, above the town on the far bank, is a medieval one which has not seen reconstruction, unlike most others along the river. It has a collection of weapons and instruments of torture.

Further on comes the little town of Boppard, with more than its fair share of impressive churches and fortifications. It is also a health spa with a wide range of hotels.

The next towns of note here are St Goar (left bank) and St Goarshausen (right bank). Frequent ferries ply between the two. Alight at St Goar for Burg Rheinfels, destroyed by the French at the end of the 18th century. In its day, this castle was one of the most formidable along the Rhine.

St Goarshausen, is the place to stop for one of the most famous of Rhine monuments, the Lorelei Rock, from whose summit, according to legends, a beautiful woman lured sailors to their deaths on the rocks with her seductive song. There is a stunning view of the Rhine Gorge from the rock, which can be reached by bus from St Goarshausen. Or you could walk...! Rhine steamers play the haunting melody of Heinrich Heine's song about the Lorelei as they sail past this place.

The village of Kaub, further south on the right bank, offers a superb view of the famous Pfalz. This white castle stands on an island in the river and was used to collect tolls from traffic until the 19th century.

We soon reach the picturesque town of Bacharach. Youth hostellers may be tempted to stay the night here as the hostel is located within the castle of Burg Stahleck.

We are now nearing the end of the Gorge. Look out for the Mouse Tower — a former customs tower and the last great monument of the trip. The river bends sharply left and is now seen on an easterly course towards Wiesbaden and Mainz. On the right bank soon after the bend is Rüdesheim, with a population of only 10,000 but the most visited town in the region. All the visitors seem to be packed into the Drosselgasse, a street where every building houses a bar! There are a number of medieval buildings of note, and a wine museum.

Your classic trip up the Rhine is now over. The train heads on towards the ancient city of Mainz, whose cathedral provides a fitting comparison with that of Cologne at the start of our trip. The train will probably not be terminating here, but the city is certainly worth a few hours of the visitor's time. The cathedral is undoubtedly impressive, and has an adjoining museum. Also worth a visit is the World Museum of Printing, devoted to Johannes Gutenberg, one of the city's sons, and the fascinating and varied old town.

From Mainz, Inter City trains continue to one or more of South Germany's major cities: Frankfurt, Karlsruhe, Freiburg, Stuttgart, Ulm and Munich, all worth a visit. Some trains continue into neighbouring Switzerland or Austria. But if you cannot continue, then you should certainly consider returning north by one of the Köln-Düsseldorfer ships. The journey is more leisurely than the train, and you really do have the time to appreciate the majestic scenery.

The Upper Mosel valley

by Peter Wakefield

The River Mosel rises in France as the Moselle and flows generally east/north-eastwards through that country into Germany to join the Rhine at Koblenz. On much of its journey through Germany it flows through a deeply incised broad valley, twisting through a series of spectacular meanders.

The steep slopes of the valley for much of its length are planted with sun-hungry vineyards. These are interspersed at frequent intervals along the valley floor with pretty villages and towns. An intricate series of well signed footpaths, as well as quiet roads, railways and often river passenger boats connect the towns and villages making it an area easy to explore for the car-less visitor. As the paths crest the valley-side there is an abrupt change of land-use to keep a quiet arable plateau land — a delight, with small fields, abundant wild flowers and many species of insect.

The Mosel Valley is easily accessible from all parts of the UK by train with an hourly high speed service to Brussels, hourly connections to Luxembourg, then approximately two-hourly connections on to Trier, in the writer's view, the best place to start a visit to this beautiful area. If you have to wait in Luxembourg explore that city too — it will be very rewarding.

Journey times are approximately:
London-Brussels:Brussels M-Luxembourg 2hrs 50 mins
Luxembourg-Trier 40 mins
Other routes to Trier are: Brussels-Cologne Inter City 2-hourly;
Cologne-Trier via Gerolstein Inter Regio 2-hourly
or via Koblenz to an hourly Koblenz-Trier Inter Regio service.

The route via Luxembourg is by and large the quickest, cheapest and certainly the most beautiful. Several of the Belgian cities en route are well worth a visit.

Trier is an elegant city, full of interest. The guide books say it is the oldest city in Germany, the Roman city at the frontier with the Barbarians. There is much Roman evidence still including the spectacular Porta Nigra, the Amphitheatre, the Basilica. There is a wide range of accommodation including a very good youth hostel next to the river, about one and a half miles from the station.

A short walking tour can be undertaken using the train and the youth hostels, most of which have excellent family accommodation. Some include en suite showers.

Day one & two: Starting at Trier, assuming Trier has been explored on the evening of day one and most of day two, take the afternoon train to Wittlich (24 minutes). From here take the railway bus from the stand adjoining the platform on which you have just alighted from the Koblenz express, to Berkastel-Kues. (The main line does not follow the valley's twists and turns but follows a more direct route, via Bullay and the Kaiser Wilhelm Tunnel, to Koblenz.)

The driver of the bus accepts the through ticket you have bought at Trier for Bernkastel-Kues and after 39 minutes or so deposits you at the terminus — the fully operational but trainless station at Bernkastel-Kues. Few people in Germany seem to use the buses that have replaced some trains. However, you are now in Kues — a pleasant enough little town but Bernkastel on the opposite bank is much prettier. Cross the bridge to Barnkastel and follow the signs up a very steep footpath to the youth hostel, about ten minutes walk. Alternatively, there is a good range of other accommodation on both sides of the river. (There is a bus to the youth hostel from Bernkastel if you cannot face the steep path)

The footpaths in the area are clearly way-marked as part of the "Regionale Wanderwege" system. An "M" indicates the paths of the Moselhöhenverbindungsweg, translatable as "Path Linking the Mosel Heights". The "M" is usually painted at appropriate points, with direction arrows painted on walls, fences, trees, stones, buildings, signposts. Occasionally it is indicated by a small metal plate. The "M" is helpfully painted en route too, to give a first-timer added confidence.

Day three: From Bernkastel-Kues it is a pleasant walk to Traben-Trarbach a few miles across the neck of a giant meander of the Mosel. From Bernkastel follow the "M" signed road/footpath through the vineyards to the summit of the valleyside, thence along and down the crest to the pleasant little riverside village of Wolf, with its good inns and restaurants. You should make it in three hours in time for lunch. It is then a gentle hour's walk past the branch railway terminus to the excellent, very modern youth hostel. A good range of other accommodation, restaurants and other facilities is available on both sides of the river.

Day four: Modern diesel trains run out of Traben station at about two-hourly intervals along the river to Bullay, with connections to Cochem, Koblenz and other towns. However, for a harder day, but very pleasant for all that, walk for part of the day en route to the next hostel at Cochem. It is

A local service train from Trier, said to be the oldest city in Germany, runs along the lush Mosel valley. Picture by John C Baker

about a four-and-a- half-hour walk, firstly down the hill from Traben Youth Hostel to the river, then downstream to Kovenig, also parallel to the railway. At Kovenig strike uphill via a quiet road to the "M" footpath system. Having gained the valley summit it is a beautiful walk, with views of the valley, through quiet woodland interspersed with meadows. Make for Alf, which can easily be reached by 2.30-3 pm. A little way up the Alf valley is an excellently equipped outdoor swimming pool. Or, you can take the foot ferry immediately for Bullay on the opposite bank of the Mosel, and then take one of the frequent trains to Cochem.

Cochem is a largish town well equipped for every sort of tourist. Train services to Koblenz are even more frequent. There are several types of river "steamer" too, plying downstream towards Koblenz. The youth hostel is on the opposite bank of the Mosel to the station, conveniently connected by a new road bridge that rises up from the station goods yard.

Day five: Using Cochem as a base for a day or so, visit the magnificent fairytale castle at Burg Eltz. This could involve taking a local train to Karden, but more pleasant in this area is to take the river steamer. Undine-Cochemer Personenschiff, for example, has a boat service leaving Cochem town centre at 10.30 arriving in Karden at 11.25. The return fare was 12DM in 1992. From Karden take the footpath "M" up the steep valleyside to the summit. Then it is a gentle two-hour stroll across beautifully quiet arable farmland by country roads, woodland paths to the castle. On top, at very nearly the end of the walk at Burg Eltz, you come to the bridge over the Elzbach. Look for the painted "M" sign and arrow at the base of the parapet. If you miss it you can waste a lot of time. Burg Eltz is family owned, very old and very spectacular. There are guided tours in English — well worth taking. It has a good cafeteria and gift shop.

The boat back to Cochem leaves Karden at 17.20 (1992). Well recommended is disembarking at Klotten, just before Cochem. Walk to the *Restaurant zu Post*, right next to the station. You can have an excellent but inexpensive meal on the terrace watching the barges on the river, and the endless succession of freight and passenger trains gliding past, just over the road. It is a pleasant walk to Cochem, (about an hour), firstly along the river, then under the railway and up the steps, along the railway, coming out at Cochem in the station yard. You will see beautiful scenery, boats, barges, and trains.

Day six: Take one of the hourly IR express trains from Cochem to Trier and back to London.

The essential map for the above walks is:
1.50000 *Topographische Karte mit Wander-und-Radwanderwegen, Die Mosel von Bernkastel-Kues bis Koblenz.*
(Landesvermessungsamt Rheinland-Pfalz)

The Hohenzollernbrücke, with Cologne's magnificent Gothic cathedral dominating the skyline in the background. Picture by R Athey

Cologne and Bonn

by Trevor Garrod

Cologne

As you emerge into the concourse of Cologne's main station, glance up through the plate glass windows and you will be impressed by the soaring spires and flying buttresses of the great Gothic cathedral of St Peter, the landmark and symbol of this 2,000-year-old city.

Traffic has been banned from most of the station forecourt and so you may proceed safely across it and up the steps or small escalator to the cathedral precinct. You will doubtless want to admire the exterior and the interior of this medieval masterpiece, dating from 1284 and finally completed in 1880, its twin spires reaching a height of 520 feet and, at the time of its completion, one of the highest buildings in the world. Then you may care to rest by the north corner and watch the mechanical clock and carillon on the building opposite as it strikes the hour.

There is much else of interest within a few minutes walk. Just to the south of the cathedral is the Roman Germanic Museum containing a Dionysius mosaic discovered on this site in 1941 during excavations for an air-raid shelter. Just beyond are two other museums that will be of interest to art lovers — the Wallraf-Richartz and Ludwig museums.

Colonia Agrippina — hence its modern name in English (Cologne) and German (Köln) — was founded by the Romans on the site of a previous Germanic settlement, and their remains can also be seen in the foundations of the Praetorium preserved under the City Hall. These were discovered when the building was being erected in 1953. Then there is the Schmitz-Column in a quiet square nearby. This column contains Roman stonework, but was actually put up on this site to mark Neil Armstrong's first steps on the moon in 1969. Streets with names like Buttermarkt and Fischmarkt bear witness to earlier activities in this old part of the city, much of it bombed in the last war but carefully and sensitively rebuilt.

You can relax at pavement cafés and restaurants around the cobbled Alter Markt or at one of those facing the gardens that line the banks of the Rhine nearby. Here you can watch the Köln-Düsseldorfer steamers arriving and departing from the small pier, the frequent trains rumbling across the river between the curved spans of the mighty Hohenzollern bridge just to the north, or the road traffic and trams crossing the graceful modern Deutz bridge just to the south. Downriver, beyond the railway bridge and on the opposite bank, is the Rhine Park and neighbouring exhibition grounds, themselves linked by cable car to the zoo, back on the same side of the Rhine as the old city.

Shoppers are well catered for in the narrow pedestrianised Hohe Strasse and Schildergasse, the former leading south from the cathedral to reach the latter. You will also see street performers and traders and hear a babble of tongues from the many international tourists in this lively city of nearly a million people. There are also several other churches from the Middle Ages to visit, sections of the city's old walls and gates, seven museums and 35 art galleries.

An efficient system of trams and buses will take you into the suburbs and surrounding area. The Verkehrsverbund Rhein-Sieg carries over 1,200,000 passengers every day, with through ticketing between different modes. For full information about services — which even includes a leaflet on suggested cycle rides from tram termini — write to the network at D5000 Köln 1, Barbarossaplatz 1. The Tourist Information Office address is Verkehrsamt, D5000 Köln 1, Am Dom — it is right next to the cathedral.

Cologne to Bonn — by tram

Near the cathedral, and at other points in the city centre, you will see large square signs with the letter "U" on them. In most large German cities, that is short for "U-bahn" or underground railway.

In several cities, what actually happened was that existing tramways were diverted into underground tunnels in central areas. Cologne followed this process between 1968 and 1970, and in subsequent years also converted some suburban sections into subways. In 1978, the Köln-Bonner Eisenbahn was integrated into the system and now the two cities and a considerable area around them are served by what has become the Rhein-Sieg Stadtbahn with a fully integrated ticketing system.

There can be few places in Europe where you can take a single tram journey from beneath one city centre to another 20 miles away.

It can be done at Cologne by catching service 16 from Dom/ Hauptbahnhof underground station. After curving through several other stations in the tunnels, the articulated vehicle comes to the surface in busy Barbarossaplatz, which is named after a 12th century emperor with a red beard, but which, with its tall modern buildings, has definitely more in common with the 20th century. It then proceeds like a normal tram on reserved track down the wide Ubierring, named after the Germanic tribe who were here before the Romans, to the stop at Marienburg. Next to it is a carpark with the large P+R sign. More than 100 stations on the conventional railway and the tram, or light rapid transit, system in the Rhine-Sieg area now have these free parking facilities, and so keep nearly 10,000 cars out of the city centres.

Marienburg is by the river, and we now glide along its banks for a time, past leafy suburbs, before veering inland through an industrial area. Here you can see sidings with freight wagons of the KBE (Köln-Bonner Eisenbahn) and other operators, for this remarkable rail system also carries diesel-hauled goods traffic on certain sections and has links to the DB main line.

There are level crossings now, as on a normal railway, and conventional stations like those serving the large suburb of Wesseling. Indeed, Urfeld station even boasts a Bahnhofs-Hotel and Restaurant. For a short spell, this even seems like a rural railway as it passes orchards and small fields.

Buschdorf station has the bright yellow canopies that are standard for public transport boarding points in and around Bonn. The line proceeds in a cutting with further stations boasting car parks and well-filled cycle sheds. After Bonn West, the tram plunges into a tunnel built between 1975 and 1979 to bring it to the Hauptbahnhof and other underground stops in the city centre and government quarter.

Bonn

Until 1948, few British people had heard of Bonn. Those that had would have been aware of it as a pleasant old university town at the northern end of the Rhine Gorge, and as the birthplace of one of

Europe's greatest composers, Ludwig van Beethoven.

When the Federal Republic of Germany was founded in 1949, out of the three western occupation zones of the country, it needed a capital, at least temporarily. For Berlin, Germany's capital since 1870, was not currently available, although the constitution of the new republic envisaged it ultimately becoming the capital of a reunited country. Bonn was chosen against competition from larger and more important centres like Frankfurt, and it is said that the influence of the Rhinelander, Konrad Adenauer, who was to become the first Chancellor of the new republic, had much to do with its selection. To draw a comparison with our country, it was rather like making Durham the capital of England and then extending the Tyne and Wear Metro to serve it!

Bonn grew from 90,000 population 40 years ago to some 296,000 today and has become a capital of world significance, although during the course of the 1990s it will gradually lose many of its functions to the reunited Berlin.

Bonn is served by all main trains on the main left bank route through the Rhine Gorge, while its suburb, Beuel, has a station on the right bank. You can also reach it by Köln-Düsseldorfer Rhine steamer. But perhaps the most interesting way to approach it is by light rapid transit from Cologne as described above.

Whether you arrive at Bonn Hauptbahnhof or at the adjacent underground station, you are already virtually in the city centre. To your right is an attractive line of public gardens leading to the orange-coloured building of the university, founded in 1777. The numbers of bicycles and the student atmosphere are a little reminiscent of Oxford and Cambridge — indeed, Bonn has an Oxfordstrasse just round the corner and is twinned with that city.

The towers of the medieval Minster dominate the large irregular Münsterplatz with the tastefully restored post office at the other end. The Minster is a simple but attractive building, contrasting with the Gothic exuberance of Cologne Cathedral. Major department stores, as well as cafés, restaurants and specialist shops, can be found here and in the neighbouring small pedestrianised streets and squares. Also of interest is the old stone gateway, the Sterntor.

Signposts lead you to Beethoven's birthplace in Bonngasse. It is a modest two-storey house that is now a museum, containing instruments, including a piano used by the composer himself, and many exhibits relating to his life and times. You may also care to rest awhile in his attractive back garden.

The Government buildings are mostly to the south of the city, which now forms a continuous built-up area upriver to Bad Godesberg. Villas have been converted to new uses and modern office blocks erected; while the Bundeshaus (Parliament building) is a large white edifice pleasantly situated by the waterside. You could take the U-bahn from

Hauptbahnhof or Universität/Markt for its run in a tunnel under Adenauer-Allee, which is effectively Germany's Whitehall.

The tram, train or LRT vehicle — whatever we care to call it — emerges into daylight near the British Embassy (on your left) and continues its run on a reserved track to Rheinallee, just 100 yards from the main line station of Bad Godesberg, itself a refined riverside spa town set against a background of hills.

Another trip on rails from the centre of Bonn is that by tram over the Kennedy Bridge to Beuel and then up the right bank to Königswinter and Bad Honnef. The former is a popular resort dominated by the Drachenfels, one of the hills of the Siebengebirge. The hill takes its name from the dragon killed by the hero Siegfried in the Dark Ages, according to the legend of the Nibelungen. Apparently these hills also have associations with Snow White and her seven dwarfs...

You can climb up the wooded slopes of the Drachenfels to the ruined castle at the summit. For the less energetic, there is also a metre-gauge rack railway which climbs 220 metres in 1.5kms. From the top, the view southwards up the Rhine valley will surely tempt you to further exploration of this fascinating part of Germany.

Bonn University, founded in 1777, gives the city an atmosphere not unlike that of its twin city, Oxford

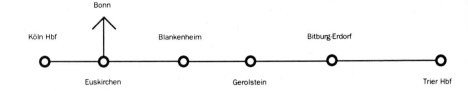

CHAPTER 13

Cologne-Trier

by Trevor Garrod

Colonia Agrippina, Confluens and Augusta Treverorum were three major cities founded 2,000 years ago by the Romans when they extended their Empire to cover western Germany.

As present-day Köln (Cologne), Koblenz and Trier, they remain important centres on the water and road networks; but you can also travel between them by main line train, following the gorges of the Rhine and Mosel. Electrification of the Koblenz-Trier line, parallel to the Mosel, in 1973 led to faster journeys and the routeing of most long-distance freight from Cologne to Trier by this longer line.

However, the Romans also liked to travel in a direct fashion, and you can do this between Cologne and Trier by taking the secondary line over the top of the Eifel uplands, often referred to as the Eifelbahn.

The diesel train from Cologne leaves the main line at Kalscheuren at the southern end of the city and crosses a flat landscape in the Cologne-Bonn commuter belt to reach Euskirchen, where another secondary line trails in from Bonn.

After Euskirchen the countryside becomes more sparsely populated. An early sign that we are approaching a different region comes as we pass the castle of Veynau, one of several on this route. Then, after Mechernich, the ascent starts in earnest as the line curves up into the hills, through pine forests, climbing over 90 metres into the tunnel at Kall. Our train continues to climb until it reaches the small station of Schmidtheim, at 553 metres above sea level the summit of the line.

Not long after comes Jünkerath, whose two island platforms were busier when it was a junction for a branch westwards into the German-speaking parts of Belgium.

We are now in quiet uplands of neat farmhouses and scattered villages amid pasture and woodland, and it is not difficult to see why this line was not one of the earliest to be built, and traffic levels have not, at least so far, justified electrification. The Eifelbahn was constructed from the northern end, reaching Kall in 1867, Gerolstein in 1870 and Trier the following year. The speed of its construction, once it started, was no doubt a result of the expansionist policies of Prussia under Bismarck at that time. In 1871, the German Empire was founded, Alsace-Lorraine was annexed from France, and this line came to play an important role in moving heavy freight between the industrial areas of Lorraine and the Ruhr.

From Jünkerath the line gradually descends and we soon reach Gerolstein, the largest town in these parts, with a population of 7,000. At 362 metres above sea level, it is classified as what Germans call a "Luftkurort" — a spa noted for its invigorating air — and its hotels and guesthouses are attractively perched on the valley sides.

The landscape now changes again as the line makes a gradual descent of the Kyll valley. The stations are often imposing buildings of local sandstone, as are many of the churches in the small towns and villages that they serve.

The valley becomes, in places, a rocky gorge, small settlements among the trees succeed one another and rocky outcrops give a more romantic flavour to the ride, especially if you spot a castle such as Burg Ramstein perched on one of the hills. One of the larger places, but still only with a 1,200 population, is Kyllburg, also a spa. Between here and Kordel the line runs through ten short tunnels and crosses the river 17 times as it follows its sinuous course.

After Kordel, the valley finally broadens for the final stretch to the Mosel, which we cross to reach Trier. It is a good centre for touring three countries by train and river steamer and its proximity to France has given it a French name, Trèves, as well as its German and Latin ones.

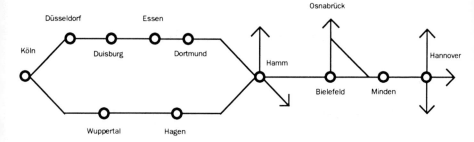

CHAPTER 14

Cologne-Berlin

by Trevor Garrod

The journey starts under the curved roof of Cologne's main station, on the banks of the Rhine, alongside the soaring spires of the great Gothic cathedral. 380 miles and seven hours later we shall see, through the same train window, the Reichstag, the Television Tower and other famous landmarks of Berlin.

The electric Inter City train is soon speeding northwards then eastwards through Düsseldorf and Duisburg, Essen and Dortmund — modern industrial cities of the Ruhr, rebuilt after the Second World War as part of the 1950s Economic Miracle.

Beyond this vast conurbation lies the agricultural plain of Westphalia, where we call at the city of Bielefeld; then we see, ahead of us, the wooded hills of the Teutoburger Wald. This is as far as the Romans could reach, 2,000 years ago, before being beaten by Arminius, also known as Herman the German.

At Löhne we thread junctions to join the east-west main line, used by trains from the Netherlands. Soon we are passing through the Porta Westfalica — an imposing gap in the hills which we share with the River Weser. Note the monument to Kaiser Wilhelm, up on the left, overlooking this strategic gateway; and the battlement architecture of Minden station, through which we shortly pass. The route from Cologne to Minden will be 150 years old in 1995.

Pleasant undulating country follows, until we draw into Hannover, a

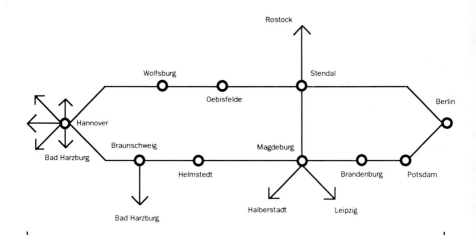

large and handsome city worth a visit in its own right, and as a centre for excursions northwards to Lüneburg Heath and southwards to the picturesque Pied Piper town of Hameln and the mysterious Harz Mountains. The beautiful towns of Goslar and Bad Harzburg, at the foot of these mountains, enjoy a good train service from Hannover. Wernigerode, the attractive town at the northern end of the Harzquerbahn (Trans-Harz Railway), one of the longest narrow-gauge steam networks in Europe, is reached by bus from Bad Harzburg or train from Magdeburg.

The next city, Braunschweig (Brunswick) is smaller but also attractive; and is followed by Helmstedt which, for 40 years, was the border town. Here, in the days of the Cold War, locomotives and crews would be changed before the train trundled forward, through the barbed wire frontier, to the village station of Marienborn. Here, flags, posters and frontier guards would announce our arrival in the German Democratic Republic, lengthy searches of the train would take place and transit visas would be issued to passengers.

Since German reunification in October 1990, things have of course changed; and a new high-speed line is now planned from Hannover to Berlin. Some of the fastest trains now use a more northerly route via Wolfsburg — home of Volkswagen — and Stendal. For the moment, however, we continue through rather bare, arable farmland, threaded by roads lined with small trees, to reach Magdeburg, an ancient city dominated by the twin towers of its cathedral.

North of the city, our train swings east to cross another great slow-moving river, the Elbe — followed by mile upon mile of flat farmland, with no towns of any significance, then increasing tracts of forest, especially birch and conifers and occasional lakes. This is Mark Brandenburg, the region of which Berlin was originally the capital.

Potsdam is the next place of interest, with its impressive views of handsome buildings mirrored in lakes to the north of the railway line. Beyond this garrison town come more thick forests, through which the barbed wire border between the former GDR and West Berlin used to run.

Then we pull into Wannsee station, serving a sandy lakeside beach popular with Berliners, before shooting straight as a die through the Grunewald, parallel with the Avus motorway. The trees give way to city suburbs and we are soon running on the Stadtbahn, an elevated four-track line snaking its way across this city of four million people. It affords grand-stand views of the radio and television towers, Gedächtniskirche ruin, zoo, Congress Hall, Tiergarten park, Victory Column and impressive modern buildings. We have a choice of stations — Zoologischer Garten, Friedrichstrasse, Hauptbahnhof — from which excellent public transport in the form of buses, S-bahn and Underground enable us to explore the city and its surrounding forests and lakes. "Berlin ist ein Besuch wert" — Berlin is worth a visit — has long been one of the city's slogans, and no-one with a feeling for 20th century history can fail to be impressed by it.

The imposing sight of the Brandenburg Gate, Berlin

CHAPTER 15

Koblenz, Ehrenbreitstein and the Lahn Valley

by Felix Schmid

Koblenz, from the Latin "confluentes", is an odd town, lying at the confluence of the rivers Rhine and Mosel. The town is situated mostly on the left bank of the Rhine, straddling the Mosel. Its imposing main station is the junction for the main Rhine Valley line, a link to the mostly freight carrying line on the right bank of the Rhine and the railway up the Mosel valley to Trier and Luxembourg. The town was badly damaged during the Second World War but its charming old centre, around the old churches of Liebfrauen, St Kastor and Florin, has been beautifully restored to its Baroque splendour. It is a Baroque town because of the devastation wrought earlier by the Thirty Years War. For a short while it was the seat of the Archbishop-electors of Trier who built the Kurfürstliches Schloss (castle) and the Stadttheater at the beginning of the 19th century.

Walking from the station to the landing stages on the left bank of the Rhine you could visit the Alte Burg, built to protect the 14th century Balduinbrucke across the Mosel, and then the centre of old Koblenz and the St Kastor Kirche, which is well worth a look. It is situated next to the Deutschordenhaus which is far more interesting than the remains of a monument to Kaiser Wilhelm I, whose ruin adorns the Deutsches Eck next to it. Walking along the Rhine we can enjoy the view across the river

The Rhine, with the Festung Ehrenbreitstein impressive in the background. Picture by Felix Schmid

towards the old Residenz of the Electors (built by Neumann at the turn of the 17th century) at the foot of the Ehrenbreitstein.

The best way to cross the river is not by railway or car but by the small ferry boat which regularly plies its trade between Koblenz and the urban zones of Pfaffendorf and Ehrenbreitstein. The river flows very fast in this relatively narrow stretch and it is an exhilarating sight to behold the little ferry rush from one side of the river to the other, narrowly missing the odd huge tanker racing downriver. There is, of course, a good reason for braving the water: on a sunny day an excursion to the Festung Ehrenbreitstein is an absolute must. Rebuilt by the Prussians in ten years from 1815, at the end of the Napoleonic wars, it is a late, and largely pointless, monument to the art of military architecture. Nevertheless it is impressive and counts as one of the world's largest fortresses.

An easy stroll from the ferry landing stage on the right bank of the Rhine brings the visitor to the foot of the rocky outcrop on which the fortress stands, dominating the Rhine, Mosel and Deutsches Eck. Signs point to the "Sessellift", or chairlift, which promises an easy ascent to the fortifications. Be warned: it takes as long to walk to the top as it takes to "burrow" through the winding tunnel which used to give access to munitions dumps and underground stores, carved out of the rock. The ride by chairlift is expensive but brief and deposits the weary traveller almost inside the walls of the citadel and close to the Rheinmuseum and the Landesmuseum. The view from the main courtyard is breathtaking, sweeping from the Taunus hills in the south, over the Hunsrück in the west to the Westerwald in the north, with the town and the two rivers laid out beneath. The fortress is well worth exploring — especially by those who are choosing to stay overnight: the Festung Ehrenbreitstein also houses the town's youth hostel.

We can return to Koblenz by bus or ferry to pick up a train heading for the Lahn valley or we can take one of the rare local stopping trains from Ehrenbreitstein halt to Niederlahnstein, the station which provides the interchange between the main line on the right bank of the Rhine and the branch line up the Lahn valley to Limburg. The former option is to be preferred since it affords a good view downriver (sit on the left of the train). The view upriver is obstructed by a huge road bridge. This is the last opportunity to see Ehrenbreitstein in its full glory and say goodbye to Koblenz and the Rhine. Beyond the bridge our small train briefly joins the main line from Wiesbaden to Köln and stops at Niederlahnstein, before turning off east into the valley of the River Lahn whose source is in the Siegerland, east of Cologne. The Lahn is not a river that can be expected to follow an obvious route for more than a few miles! It twists and turns and seems bent on visiting exciting places, such as Marburg, Giessen, Wetzlar and Limburg.

Looking up to the right we can catch a brief glimpse of Burg Lahneck, which overlooks the rivers Rhine and Lahn and the motorway. The valley immediately captivates the visitor. It is what Germans call "lieblich" — pretty and loveable. At the same time it forms a transport corridor boasting a navigable river, railway and road links. Its importance has declined though over the years and both river and railway have taken on the rôle of catering for the leisure market. The railway is still partly double track, an indication of its earlier importance but most stations have been reduced to the bare minimum. The river meanders between cliffs and woods, with the occasional caravan park on its banks. There are sawmills and old factories here and there, usually close to locks and wharves on the canal river, which provide an incongruous sight in this rural valley.

The small villages all look prosperous and well kept. As the valley widens we briefly stop at Nievern, and are obviously still in the commuter area of Koblenz. Shortly afterwards we reach Bad Ems, an expensive spa town with many fine fin-de-siècle hotels with the "Russischer Hof" (Russian town) on the opposite bank of the Lahn visible from the train. The town is famous for the events that led to the creation of German national unity and the Franco-German War in 1870. King Wilhelm I of Prussia had been taking the waters and was visited by the French ambassador who wanted an assurance that Germany would not intervene in Spain. Bismarck then used this to create a diplomatic incident which led the French to declare war, with terrible consequences.

After the goods yard at Bad Ems station the valley narrows, and beyond a lock and weir we pass Dausenau. The river bends to the left, looking just like a quiet pond with the remains of terraced vineyards above it. The railway becomes single track here before crossing a traditional arched steel bridge to enter Nassau (Lahn), whose one claim to fame is its association with the German dynasty of Oranien-Nassau. The valley is now really lovely and green as we travel upriver on the right bank. As the cliffs close in on the river the railway is forced to tunnel through a rocky outcrop, bypassing a lock on the river and emerging to a backdrop of the twin spires of Obernhof church. There are another two short tunnels and a river crossing before we reach Obernhof (Lahn) halt, still protected by semaphore signals. On leaving Obernhof you may see swans on this tranquil stretch of the river before entering a longer tunnel which brings us out into a narrow gorge.

The landscape becomes more and more rocky, with forested slopes on both banks. On a sunny day trees are reflected in the water and the old linesmen's houses show themselves to great advantage. Above Laurenburg on the left look for a medieval tower. The valley becomes just wide enough to squeeze in a football pitch before it turns once more into a rocky gorge. At Laurenburg the Lahn Ferienstrasse (tourist route) leaves railway and river — there is not enough space for all three! The Lahn power station is on our left as we enter a tunnel which cuts off a long, almost 360-degree, bend in the river. On leaving the tunnel, look to the right for a ruined fortress which announces the village of Balduinstein with its quaint old station. Again we cross the river before passing through two more tunnels and, finding ourselves between plantation forests and "Auenwälder", the woods on the side of the river. Facingen (Lahn) is a striking-looking village built on a rocky outcrop and is the last stop before Diez, the seat of one of the offshoots of the Oranien-Nassau family. Their impressive and distinctive medieval castle reaches into the sky with its clock tower, high above the town's old streets. The schloss (castle) has been turned into a youth hostel and the area is well worth exploring, perhaps taking in the Baroque Schloss Oranienstein.

A few kilometres further on we cross the boundary of Rhineland-Palatinate into Hessen and approach Limburg (Lahn) station. Just before the station the line is again under the wires of electrification which we had left behind at Niederlahnstein. Do not overlook the semi-circular locomotive shed with its clock tower. The town of Limburg is most famous for a particularly pungent type of cheese, the Limburger, best eaten with Kümmel seeds. It is dominated by the cathedral on a rocky spur above the river. Built in the first half of the 13th century this resembles a 19th century imitation of a Gothic building. But it is the genuine article. The castle next to it is a fortified complex dating back to the ninth century. Below castle and cathedral is the Altstadt, the virtually intact medieval centre of town. There are many venerable half-timbered houses around Fischmarkt, including the historic Rathaus, a well preserved 14th century Gothic building.

In Limburg we are spoilt for choice. We can continue our journey east up the River Lahn to Weilburg, with its 16th century schloss, to Wetzlar and Giessen, north to Siegburg and south to Wiesbaden/Mainz and Frankfurt. All these options lead through pleasant countryside on well served lines.

Mannheim

by Felix Schmid

Mannheim Haupbahnhof is familiar to many rail travellers heading south or east in Germany as it is the interchange for the country's synchronised arrivals and departures of Inter City trains. Every hour two trains arrive from different routes and passengers can easily transfer from one to the other. Mannheim the town, however, tends to be neglected.

Glanced at from the train, Mannheim is rather unprepossessing: railway and roads conspire to cut off the town from one of its main features, the River Rhine which, together with its tributary, the Neckar, was the reason for its foundation in 1606.

In 1720 Mannheim was made the main seat of the court of the County Palatine and Count Carl Philipp ordered it to be laid out as a planned town, orientated towards his schloss, the largest Baroque palace ever built in Germany. Although badly damaged during the Second World War, the outside of the palace and the chapel have been beautifully restored and are now part of Mannheim University. The town was the seat of the court for 57 years and was totally rebuilt during this period.

The town within the walls was laid out in a grid square with 144 blocks, labelled alpha-numerically, starting with A1 from one wing of the palace and L1 from the other.

The old town is today encircled by a four-segment ring, the site of the old fortifications, reminiscent of Parisian boulevards.

At the south-east end of the old town we find the Wasserturm, or water tower, which is one of Mannheim's main features. Built at the beginning of the fin-de-siècle or Jugendstil (Art Nouveau) period, late in the 19th century, it is now the focal point of the Friedrichsplatz, with its ponds and fountains. Only a short walk from this pleasant place is the Kunsthalle with one of the best German collections of 19th and 20th century sculpture and painting. This includes one of the four versions, perhaps the best, of Manet's *Execution of Emperor Maximilian of Mexico*.

Near the point where the Luisenring, Friedrichsring and Kurpfalzbrücke meet is the departure point for harbour cruises as well as the Navigation Museum housed in the 1920s steamer, *Mainz*, and the terminus of the OEG, Oberrheinische Eisenbahngesellschaft, the interurban tramway to Heidelberg at the foot of the Odenwald. Walking upriver along the southern bank of the Neckar we reach the Fernmeldeturm, a TV and communications tower with a rotating restaurant giving a superb view of the town and the surrounding countryside.

Key railway vocabulary

English	French	German	Dutch
railway	chemin de fer	(Eisen) bahn	spoorweg
train	train	Zug	trein
station	gare	Bahnhof	station
waiting room	salle d'attente	Wartezimmer	wachtkamer
luggage	bagages	Gepäck	bagage
toilet	toilette	Toilette	toilet
Gentlemen	messieurs	Herren	heren
Ladies	mesdames	Damen	dames
reservations	réservations	Platzkarten	reserveringen
tickets	billets	Fahrkarten	kaartjes
single	aller / simple	Einfach	enkele reis
return	aller et retour	hin und zurück	retour
1st class	première classe	erste Klasse	eerste Klas
standard class	seconde classe	zweite Klasse	tweede Klas
restaurant car	wagon-restaurant	Speisewagen	restauratiewagen
sleeping car	wagon-lits	Schlafwagen	slaapwagen
couchette car	wagon de couchettes	Liegewagen	couchette
showers	douches	Duschen	douches
platform	quai	Bahnsteig	perron
		(Gleis: one side of platform)	(spoor: one side of platform)
timetable	horaire (poster)	Fahrplan (poster)	dienstregeling (poster)
	indicateur (book)	Kursbuch (book)	spoorboek (book)
underground	Métro	U- Bahn	metro
reduction	réduction	Ermässigung	verkorting
supplement	supplément	Zuschlag	toeslag
one must	il faut	man muss	men moet
reserve	réserver	reservieren	reserveren
change	changer	umsteigen	overstappen
forbidden	défense de interdit de	verboten	verboden
smoking	fumeur	rauchen	Roken
arrival	arrivée	Ankunft	ankomst
departure	départ	Abfahrt	vertrek
steam	vapeur	Dampf	stoom
diesel railcar	autorail	Triebwagen	motorrijtuig
locomotive	locomotive	Lok (omotive)	locomotief

Key words and abbreviations

The national railway network in each country is known by its initials:

FRANCE:	SNCF — Société nationale de chemins de fer français.
BELGIUM:	SNCB — Société nationale de chemins de fer belges.
	NMBS — Nationaal Maatschappij der Belgische Spoorwegen.
LUXEMBOURG:	CFL — Chemins de fer luxembourgeois
NETHERLANDS:	NS — Nederlandse Spoorwegen
GERMANY:	DB — Deutsche Bundesbahn*
	DR — Deutsche Reichsbahn*

*The DB and DR were the national railway companies of the former West and East German states respectively. Since reunification in 1990 they have worked more closely together and merged into DBAG (Deutsche Bahn AG) on January 1, 1994.

In France:
(TGV) Train à Grande Vitesse — High Speed Train
Composter un billet — to validate a ticket (by special machine at entrance to platform)

In Germany:
ICE — InterCity Express
EC — Eurocity (also in neighbouring countries) fast train
D-Zug — fast train
A supplement is payable on all of these trains

Inter Regio — fast inter-regional train catering for a market similar to Express Sprinters in Great Britain.
Eilzug — "hurrying train", semi-fast train
Nahverkehrszug / Personenzug — local stopping train
S-bahn — suburban train
Hauptbahnhof — main station

Refreshments: on continental trains, refreshment trolleys are common, selling hot and cold drinks, sandwiches etc. Some trains carry a buffet car or bistro car instead of a full restaurant car.

All the more important stations have a restaurant, buffet, café or bar and often a range of shops including one where you can buy bread, rolls, cold drinks etc to take with you. (In German stations, look for the sign *Reiseproviant* for this.)

Miles and kilometres: The metric system is used in all the continental countries in this book. A simple rule-of-thumb conversion guide is that 5 miles are approximately 8 kilometres; to convert kilometres to miles multiply by 5 and then divide by 8.

More foreign words: In 1993 Thomas Cook published the *European Rail Traveller's Phrasebook* (ISBN 0 906273 39 0) at £3.95. It contains over 300 useful phrases in nine languages including French and German but not Dutch.

Further information

Many guidebooks, and series of guidebooks, are available covering the countries of this book. These guides often contain competent descriptions of major towns and cities that will assist the rail traveller; they do, however, often assume that the journey there, and exploration of the surrounding area, will be by car.

The Rough Guide series is one of the most useful for the visitor using public transport and, indeed, without too much money to spend. Seven of its current titles cover the area of this book. The series is published by Rough Guides Ltd, 1 Mercer Street, London, WC2H 9QJ and distributed by Penguin.

Platform Five Publishing issues a series of European Rail Handbooks which are ideal for the visitor interested in the train on which he or she is travelling as well as the places through which it passes. They contain a wealth of information on railway locomotives and rolling stock, general hints on rail travel and a list of railway museums and preserved lines.

Ian Allan has published a series of European Railway Atlases, showing all routes, stations and depots, passenger and freight, in the countries covered by this book. For details, contact Ian Allan Ltd, Coombelands House, Coombelands Lane, Addlestone, Weybridge, Surrey, KT15 1HY.

At the time of writing, it is assumed that British Rail's all line timetable from October 1994 will include Channel Tunnel trains.

The most reliable and comprehensive reference work for train travellers abroad is the Thomas Cook European Timetable. It is published, in English, every month, and contains all the more important routes and stations throughout Europe, together with background information. For this timetable and other useful publications contact Thomas Cook, at PO Box 227, Peterborough, PE3 6SB.

Continental bookings can be made at the International Rail Centre, Victoria Station, London, SW1V 1JY (Tel: 071-834-2345 for inquiries). Major stations and many BR-appointed travel agents can also take bookings, and the Railway Development Society has been pressing for more such outlets.

The countries featured in this book all maintain tourist offices in London and, in some cases, the national rail systems also have an office:

FRANCE:	**Railways**: 179 Piccadilly, London W1V 9DB ☎ **071-491-2573**
	Tourist Office: 178 Piccadilly, London W1V 9DB ☎ **071-499-6911**
GERMANY:	**Railways**: 18 Conduit Street, London W1R 9TD ☎ **071-499-0577**
	Tourist Office: Nightingale House, 65 Curzon Street, London W1Y 7PE ☎ **071-495-3990**
BELGIUM:	**Railways**: 439 Premier House, 10 Greycoat Place, London SW1P 1SB ☎ **071-233-0360**
	Tourist Office: Premier House, Gayton Rd, Harrow, Middx ☎ **081-861-3300**
NETHERLANDS:	**Railways**: Egginton House, Buckingham Gate, London SW1E 6LD ☎ **071-630-1735**
	Tourist Office: *same address* ☎ **071-630-0451**
LUXEMBOURG:	**Tourist Office**: 122 Regent Street, London W1 ☎ **071-434-2800**
SWITZERLAND:	**Tourist Office**: 1 New Coventry Street, London W1 ☎ **071-734-1921**

WHAT IS THE RAILWAY DEVELOPMENT SOCIETY?

The Railway Development Society (RDS) is the only national pro-rail pressure group independent of both rail management and unions. It was formed in 1978 by the amalgamation of two long-established voluntary associations and today acts as campaigner for a fairer share of transport investment in the railways of this country, and as a consumer organisation representing rail issues nationwide. It is not linked with any political party, and has members of all shades of political opinion.

We seek a better rail system for Britain because we believe that railways offer a safer and more fuel-efficient alternative to the uncontrolled growth of road transport for passengers and freight. We are very concerned at the effects of road transport on the environment and believe that much greater use of rail transport is the best means of reducing pollution, conserving fuel, reducing noise and helping to improve quality of life in the community. We are not anti-car; most of our members are car-owners, but we believe that it is necessary to provide an acceptable alternative for many journeys. Nor are we anti-lorry as we recognise the part played by the lorry in the nation's economy. Nevertheless, we question the price we have to pay — particularly for the heavy long-distance lorry on our roads.

We have campaigned with some success for further electrification of the rail network, for better local and regional trains, and for the reopening of stations and lines closed to passengers. We have strongly opposed rail cuts and closures, and continue to do so. We have also done much detailed work in helping to promote the transfer of freight traffic from road to rail, and have successfully supported a number of grant applications under Section 8 of the Railways Act 1974. The Channel Tunnel, a vital link with the rest of the European railway network, is a project which we have always supported, and we are delighted to see it completed. We now want to see the provision of appropriate rail routes to it from the whole of the country.

As a consumer organisation we provide a voice for rail users, both passengers and freight, and companies involved in wagon manufacture and similar trades. We speak up for their interests with ministers, national and local politicians and rail management, all of whom take far-reaching decisions affecting rail users' everyday lives. We have made specific representations in order to prevent deterioration in services and to ensure improvements wherever possible. We also act as a national advisory body for the many local rail users' groups.

Our quarterly journal *Railwatch* is read by many interested parties outside as well as inside the society, as are our local branch newsletters. We also publish books and leaflets on particular issues, and a series of regional guidebooks for rail passengers which has become widely popular with the travelling public.

As a voluntary body, financed almost entirely from individual subscriptions and donations, we have made sure that the case for rail is heard, and are determined to continue pressing for a better future for rail transport in this country.

Further information about the Railway Development Society may be obtained from the Administrative Officer, Railway Development Society, 48 The Park, Great Bookham, Surrey KT23 3LS (0372 52863).

Trevor Garrod,
May 1994